HUMANISM AND THE ABSURD
IN THE MODERN NOVEL

Humanism
and the Absurd
in the
Modern Novel

NAOMI LEBOWITZ

 Northwestern University Press

Evanston, 1971

Naomi Lebowitz is Associate Professor of English and Comparative Literature at Washington University in St. Louis.

For Joel and Judith

"To believe in the existence of human beings as such is love," says Simone Weil. This is what makes the difference. It is possible—all too possible—to say when we have read one more modern novel: "So what? What do I care? You yourself, the writer, didn't really care." It is all too often like that. But this caring or believing or love alone matters. All the rest, obsolescence, historical views, manners, agreed views of the Universe, is simply nonsense and trash. If we don't care, don't immediately care, then perish books both old and new, and novelists, and governments too. If we do care, if we believe in the existence of others, then what we write is necessary.

Saul Bellow

 CONTENTS

INTRODUCTION

THIS BOOK is, in effect, an apology for a humanism that finds its expression mainly in an "old" form of the modern novel, a form that is generally considered dead or dying because its traditional habitat has vanished. Saul Bellow's war on critics is based on his feeling that they are seeking to translate the humanist's novel out of existence by insisting that it depends on conventions that are no longer intact, reality having fundamentally and radically altered. Their argument goes that those novelists who yearn for an old order no longer have the necessary historical stage to stand upon, that Stendhal's mirror on the roadway now reflects a new order that can be portrayed only by a "new" novel, which, for want of a more precise generic term, I shall refer to hereafter as absurdist.

Even those critics who wish to salvage the humanist novel are led to historicize its intentions. They attempt to preserve literary humanism by transcending it, by making art either a historical climax or a substitute for religion. Claude Lévi-Strauss's comment at the end of *The Savage Mind* is pertinent:

> We need only recognize that history is a method . . . to reject the equivalence between the notion of humanity which some

have tried to foist on us with the unavowed aim of making historicity the last refuge of a transcendental humanism.[1]

The identification of the function of literature with that of religion, coming to us from Romanticism and filtered through Matthew Arnold and George Eliot, has by now been explored by almost every major critic. In his introduction to D. H. Lawrence's *Psychoanalysis and the Unconscious*, Philip Rieff describes the psychological basis for this assumption:

> Through the mediation of a writer, painter, composer, movie director, the work of art is experienced as a thing in itself, bracketed and raised above the ordinary workaday world, yet related to that world as revelation is related to that which is revealed—superior and saving.[2]

Nothing could be more threatening to the life of the humanist's novel than the tendency of sympathetic critics to take for granted its dependence on a certain form or a certain world. In spite of distracting modern atmospheres, the humanist still writes novels; his temperament refuses to be controlled by projections of intellectual, cultural, aesthetic, or metaphysical orders, though, as T. S. Eliot claims, the humanist feeds on them parasitically.[3]

Two attitudes—one associated with the "old" humanist novel, the other with the "new" absurdist fiction—will, in the course of this study, be developed from an intensive examination of a relatively small number of books that clearly profit from such treatment. This is not to imply that other books could not have been used as well. I am not presuming to offer an all-embracing theory of the modern novel or a methodological superstructure, but rather am interested in tracing two significant and contrasting tones that have remained substantially constant through changes of political and social atmospheres. Because of this constancy,

1. Claude Lévi-Strauss, *The Savage Mind*, trans. George Weidenfeld (Chicago: Univ. of Chicago Press, 1966), p. 262.
2. Philip Rieff, "Introduction," in *Psychoanalysis and the Unconscious* by D. H. Lawrence (New York: Viking, 1960).
3. T. S. Eliot, "The Humanism of Irving Babbitt," in *Selected Essays* (New York: Harcourt, Brace & Co., 1950), pp. 420–21.

little can be gained by discussing at length the particular social or political forces surrounding the novels. To explore the problems of Flaubert's bourgeois monarchy as distinguished from the Victorian pressures of George Eliot's day or the czarist repressions of Dostoevsky's time would be digressive.

It is valuable to present and define initially the essential qualities of humanist and absurdist temperaments in a more crystallized and epigrammatic form than they ordinarily take in fiction. For this reason, in Chapter One, while making other references where useful, I primarily set the humanist confessions of Montaigne against those of Dostoevsky's absurdist underground man. After then examining Flaubert's early mastery of the absurdist use of the novel, I concentrate on major humanist novels that struggle with the two directions within their own confines: *Daniel Deronda, A Passage to India,* and *The Brothers Karamazov.* In the final chapter, I compare representative twentieth-century absurdist novels with those of other contemporary writers who, though employing absurdist forms, maintain the humanist tone. I have, along the way, deliberately crossed well-traveled territory—the problem of the "Jewish half" of *Daniel Deronda,* the question of Flaubert's aesthetic coldness, the negativism of Forster's humanism, the persistence of Dostoevsky's transvaluating energy. My intention is not to invent but, by means of a fresh perspective, to recapture the vital and enduring sense of the novel's humanism.

As for the absurdists, by making them appear to be the victims of my apology for humanism, I do not mean to imply that major novels have not been and will not be produced by them. I suppose I am paying them the compliment of confessing that they, at least for the present, do not need an apology.

Acknowledgment

I would like to thank the American Association of University Women for granting me the Susan B. Riley Fellowship for 1966–67, which enabled me to begin work on this book.

HUMANISM AND THE ABSURD
IN THE MODERN NOVEL

It is a pity that . . . man cannot be at the same time impressive and truthful.

E. M. Forster

CHAPTER ONE

Two Philosophies of the Absurd

I 'VE KNOWN so many of them! says Sartre's Roquentin in an angry indictment of humanists:

> The radical humanist is the particular friend of officials. The so-called "left" humanist's main worry is keeping human values; he belongs to no party because he does not want to betray the human, but his sympathies go towards the humble. . . . He is generally a widower with a fine eye always clouded with tears: he weeps at anniversaries. He also loves cats, dogs, and all the higher mammals. The Communist writer has been loving men since the second Five-Year Plan; he punishes because he loves. Modest as all strong men, he knows how to hide his feelings, but he also knows, by a look, an inflection of his voice, how to recognize, behind his rough and ready justicial utterances, his passion for his brethren. The Catholic humanist, the late-comer, the Benjamin, speaks of men with a marvellous air. What a beautiful fairy tale, says he, is the humble life of a London dockhand, the girl in the shoe factory! He has chosen the humanism of the angels; he writes, for their edification, long, sad and beautiful novels which frequently win the Prix Femina.[1]

---

1. Jean-Paul Sartre, *Nausea*, trans. Lloyd Alexander (New York: New Directions, 1964), pp. 116–17.

These are the more easily caricatured roles that come to Roquentin's mind. But even less obviously offensive humanist positions are denounced: those of the

> humanist philosopher who bends over his brothers like a wise elder brother who has a sense of his responsibilities, the humanist who loves men as they are, the humanist who loves men as they ought to be, the one who wants to save them with their consent and the one who will save them in spite of themselves, the one who wants to create new myths, and the one who is satisfied with the old ones, the one who loves death in man, the one who loves life in man, the happy humanist who always has the right word to make people laugh, the sober humanist whom you meet especially at funerals or wakes. They all hate each other: as individuals, naturally not as men.[2]

If humanism currently is in disrepute, these varieties suggest the cause. They rehearse and simplify response to human personality; they abstract individual possibility; they sentimentalize by transcending. Kierkegaard and Dostoevsky were particularly outraged by the reductive character of humanisms which, whether based on political, religious, or moral imperatives, require a faceless crowd to justify their purpose.

Kierkegaard insists that the only organ of truth is the individual:

> There is a view of life which conceives that where the crowd is, there also is the truth, and that in truth itself there is need of having the crowd on its side. There is another view of life which conceives that wherever there is a crowd there is untruth, so that (to consider for a moment the extreme case), even if every individual, each for himself in private, were to be in possession of the truth, yet in case they were all to get together in a crowd—a crowd to which any sort of *decisive* significance is attributed, a voting, noisy, audible crowd—untruth would at once be in evidence.[3]

2. *Ibid.,* p. 117.
3. Kierkegaard, *The Point of View for My Works as an Author,* trans. Walter Lowrie (New York: Harper & Row, 1962), p. 110.

The crowd is untruth because it allows the individual who follows it to be "impenitent and irresponsible." So Christ repels the crowd, "would not found a party, did not permit balloting, but would be what He is, the Truth, which relates itself to the individual."[4]

Dostoevsky's Grand Inquisitor is a captain of the crowd, a denier of the "category of the individual."[5] And, again, it is Christ who refuses to patronize men by giving them signs and ceremonies or by allowing dreams of love for mankind to paralyze active love for one's neighbor. Although metaphysical paths to man's salvation go skyward, neither Kierkegaard nor Dostoevsky was willing to leave the earth behind. The grounding of the highest spiritual aspirations in individual responsibility, a major source of power in both writers, radically distinguishes them from Roquentin's humanists.

As one consequence of their philosophical positions, both of these writers invented characters—Kierkegaard's seducer and Dostoevsky's underground man—who, in pursuit of their own brands of truth, play out the "aesthetic category" of the interesting in order to distract themselves, by intellectual acrobatics, from the knowledge that they are unable to love a single human being.[6] Though despising mankind instead of loving it, though seeking to punish it instead of to save it, these characters, with attitudes more characteristic of the absurdist than of their authors, have in common with Roquentin's humanists not only a thirst for spiritual superiority but the inability to be redeemed by the "sense of a face." In this curious way, by starting at opposite poles, Roquentin's humanists and the absurdist come together to make an

---

4. *Ibid.*, pp. 112, 114.

5. This is one of Kierkegaard's key categories which appears throughout his writings, most particularly in *Point of View*.

6. Dostoevsky's underground man is the hero of *Notes from Underground*, ed. and trans. Ralph Matlaw (New York: E. P. Dutton, 1960). Kierkegaard's seducer is the hero of the "Diary of the Seducer," in *Either/Or*, trans. D. F. and L. M. Swenson (Princeton: Princeton Univ. Press, 1949), Vol. I; the "aesthetic category" of the interesting is explained in the same volume.

abstraction of love, and, as we shall see, become useful antitheses to the novel's humanism.

Camus defines the absurd as "the confrontation of the irrational and the wild longing for clarity whose call echoes in the human heart."[7] His humanist (and he too has caricatured the utopian humanist) is one who, recognizing the inescapability of this atmosphere, refuses to "draw any advantage from it."[8] It is in this sense that the humanist novel is characterized in the succeeding chapters. Those who attempt to heal the rift between actuality and aspiration by overcoming it, competing with it, or covering it up with metaphysical or aesthetic compensations are possessed by the absurd and feel compelled to draw advantage from it instead of merely taking it into account. This attitude is defined in the course of the book as absurdist, and it becomes readily apparent that, while the transformation of a utopian humanist into an absurdist requires merely that the absurd be revealed to him, the absurd is no stranger to the humanist novel.

From this angle, novelists like Flaubert and Proust, for whom the most important function of a decadent world is to serve as subject matter of a novel through which they alone can be liberated, may be termed absurdists. The major works of novelists as disparate as George Eliot, Dostoevsky, and Tolstoy, providing no such relief to their authors, force them to confront the absurd as humanists. Though Camus is popularly referred to as an absurdist, in this perspective he is a humanist. His undisguised obsession with the absurd, not his attitude toward it, has conventionally labeled him.

A philosophy of literary humanism is most clearly expressed in the attitudes of Montaigne, to whom George Eliot, Forster, and Gide have all paid tribute. The essayist's refusal to be seduced by abstract visions attracts these humanist novelists, and his repudia-

7. Albert Camus, *The Myth of Sisyphus*, trans. Justin O'Brien (New York: Random House, 1959), p. 16.
8. See Camus, *Notebooks, 1942–1951*, trans. Justin O'Brien (New York: Knopf, 1965), pp. 61–62.

tion of "the purity to will one thing" [9] pits him less equivocally than Kierkegaard against transcendental utopianism. Kierkegaard's emphasis on individuality is useful to the novel's humanism, but it remains largely motivated by an absurdist desire for and expectation of an ultimate truth. Thus Kierkegaard lies, masquerades, and fictionalizes to "deceive men . . . into the truth," [10] while Montaigne is more interested in luring men away from the notion of truth or any other dominating abstraction. He considers lying to be neither a weapon nor a curse, but a human condition. George Eliot admires Montaigne because

> [it seems to him] much less of a prodigy that men should lie, or that their imaginations should deceive them, than that a human body should be carried through the air on a broomstick, or up a chimney by some unknown spirit. He thinks it a sad business to persuade oneself that the test of truth lies in the multitude of believers. . . . Ordinarily, he has observed, when men have something stated to them as a fact, they are more ready to explain it than to inquire whether it is real. [11]

Montaigne admits: "I often hazard sallies of my mind which I mistrust and certain verbal subtleties at which I shake my ears; but I let them run at a venture." [12] Dostoevsky, echoing Kierkegaard, writes in his *Winter Notes:* "But my friends, I warned you in the first chapter of these notes that perhaps I would tell frightful lies, did I not? So let me be. You probably realize also that if I lie, I do so in the conviction that I am not lying." [13] Dostoevsky as essayist is concerned with transvaluating for the sake of truth. As we shall see, Dostoevsky as novelist denies himself this luxury.

---

9. This is Kierkegaard's phrase and the title of one of his discourses.

10. Kierkegaard, *Point of View,* p. 39.

11. George Eliot, "The Influence of Rationalism," in *Essays of George Eliot,* ed. Thomas Pinney (New York: Columbia Univ. Press, 1963), p. 407.

12. *The Complete Essays of Montaigne,* trans. Donald M. Frame (Stanford: Stanford Univ. Press, 1958), pp. 720–21. Future references will be to this edition and will be noted in the text.

13. Dostoevsky, *Winter Notes on Summer Impressions,* trans. R. L. Renfield (New York: McGraw-Hill, 1965), p. 88.

No concept of truth or other ultimate moral imperative can camouflage or soothe the sense of the absurd for the humanist. When Forster elects Montaigne as one of his lawgivers, he explains:

> Faith, to my mind, is a stiffening process, a sort of mental starch, which ought to be applied as sparingly as possible. I dislike the stuff. I do not believe in it, for its own sake, at all. Herein I probably differ from most people, who believe in Belief, and are only sorry they cannot swallow even more than they do. My law givers are Erasmus and Montaigne, not Moses and St. Paul. My temple stands not upon Mount Moriah but in that Elysian Field where even the immoral are admitted. My motto is: "Lord, I disbelieve—help thou my unbelief." [14]

Montaigne's humanism is decidedly not what Camus calls "the philosophy that disbelieves in pestilence." [15] He sees historical systems and predictions only as rationalizations against the plague. He dismisses belief in the infinite capacity of man's reason or the divine origin of his will, and in the unpredictable he finds the human. With the humanist's indulgence of our nature and history, Montaigne can appreciate that "wisdom [can be] less wise than madness . . . our dreams worth more than our reasonings" (p. 427). His essays reflect his recognition of the absurdity of life's forms as well as of its logic. His confessions are "grotesque and monstrous bodies, pieced together of divers members, without definite shape, having no order, sequence, or proportion other than accidental" (p. 135). Yet this view recoils from Dostoevsky's absurdist claim—"What most people regard as fantastic and lacking in universality, *I* hold to be the inmost essence of truth"— which makes of human inconsistency a transcendental sign.[16]

14. Forster, "What I Believe," in *Two Cheers for Democracy* (New York: Harcourt, Brace & Co., 1951), p. 67.

15. Camus, *The Plague*, trans. Stuart Gilbert (New York: Random House, 1948), p. 35.

16. Dostoevsky to Nikolay Nikolayevitch Strachov, Feb. 26, 1869, *Letters of Fyodor Dostoevsky*, trans. E. C. Mayne (New York: McGraw-Hill, 1964), p. 167.

Montaigne faces the absurd without this compulsive desire, and the humility of his expectation for humanism is the most central quality of his legacy to the novel. Sainte-Beuve illustrates this direction with a famous contrast. While Montaigne is amused at the spectacle of man's folly, Pascal, mocking reason, is motivated by the absurdist suspicion that "man, however wretched, is an exiled monarch, of the noblest lineage, and it behooves him to regain his rightful place." [17] Montaigne rejects any recognition as redemptive. The demand for perfection, which exorcises its frustration by witty dialectic and shuns the commonplace for a leap into the supernatural or daemonic synthesis, is not his statement or style. Montaigne's antitheses, in which he plays great against small, never annihilate what Gide calls the "purgatory of judgment."

Montaigne is at home only in this world. "Between ourselves," he says to his reader, "these are two things that I have always observed to be in singular accord: supercelestial thoughts and subterranean conduct" (p. 856). He lingers in the present: "My plan is everywhere divisible; it is not based on great hopes; each day's journey forms an end. And the journey of my life is conducted in the same way" (p. 747). With no great hopes, there is no great need for self-pity.

While Dostoevsky's absurdist underground man laments in self-justification that "for many years we have not been begotten by living fathers," [18] Montaigne endorses those ancients who, "without getting excited and without goading themselves, make themselves sufficiently felt: they have matter enough for laughter everywhere, they don't have to tickle themselves" (p. 299). The humor with which Montaigne accepts his own fathers and frailties links him to other men, just as the absurdist's rejection of both, with a compensatory rhetoric of wit that exposes human weakness

17. Charles Sainte-Beuve, "Montaigne," in *Sainte-Beuve: Selected Essays,* ed. and trans. Francis Steegmuller and Norbert Gutterman (New York: Doubleday, 1963), p. 24.
18. Dostoevsky, *Notes from Underground,* p. 115.

without indulging it, leads to the strategy of self-punishment to prosecute society.

Montaigne can pardon himself by socializing himself:

> How many stupid things I say and reply every day, in my own judgment; and so assuredly how many more in the judgment of others! If I bite my lips over them, what must the others do? In short, we must live among the living, and let the river flow under the bridge (p. 709).

Having renounced his brothers, the absurdist is compelled to celebrate his own inadequacies. He exorcises his social humiliation by inversions and transvaluations in the name of a higher conscience. "I know, I know," says the underground man, "I'm just a chatterbox, a harmless, boring chatterbox like all my kind. But how can I help it if it is the inescapable fate of every intelligent man to chatter, like filling an empty glass from an empty bottle." [19] Kierkegaard raises self-denigration to a cultural martyrdom: "In an ironical generation (that great aggregation of fools) there remains nothing else for the ironical man to do but to invert the relationship and himself become the target for the irony of all men." [20]

Because Montaigne resists making metaphysical judgments, he does not lacerate himself with repentance: "My conscience is content with itself—not as the conscience of an angel or a horse, but as the conscience of a man" (p. 612). Intoxicated with the perspective of heavens and hells, the absurdist is, like Nietzsche's representative of slave morality, "past master in . . . not forgetting, . . . in provisional self-depreciation and self-abasement." [21] He is not amused by his own falls from grace (though he often pretends to be).

Absurdist dreams of permanence and perfection climax in a

19. *Ibid.*, p. 104.
20. Kierkegaard, *Point of View*, pp. 62–63.
21. Nietzsche, "The Genealogy of Morals," in *The Philosophy of Nietzsche*, trans. Oscar Levy, ed. Geoffrey Clive (New York: New American Library, 1965), p. 412.

paralyzing sensuous devotion to an uncommon truth, garishly dressed in proud equivocations. The self is impelled to a burlesque of exhibitionism. Convention frees the humanist to search for his individuality, but it traps the absurdist in his skin. In externals, Montaigne follows "accepted fashions and forms" (p. 86), for they are the agents of husbanding the self. The absurdist's external eccentricity dehumanizes his emotions. Rousseau's boast "At least I am different" makes us suspicious, while Montaigne's profession that he shares the same soul as Caesar and the chambermaid recalls us to his uniqueness. It is, in fact, this transmogrifying "plagiarism" that so delights Gide. He speaks of Montaigne's

> rare and extraordinary propensity. . . towards listening to and even espousing other people's opinions to the point of letting them prevail over his own.[22]

He comments at another time:

> In his frequentation of the ancients, Montaigne compares himself to the bees, which "pillage the flowers here and there" but afterward turn them into honey, "completely their own"—it is no longer, he says, "thyme or marjoram."
> No, it is Montaigne, and so much the better.[23]

Ordering his public comedy of the self through conversation and example, Montaigne moves easily between the outer and inner worlds, but quite the opposite is true of the absurdist, of whose talking Kafka asks:

> Would you call it a conversation if the other person is silent and, to keep up the appearance of a conversation, you try to substitute for him and so imitate him, and so parody him, and so parody yourself?[24]

22. André Gide, "Presenting Montaigne," trans. Dorothy Bussy, in *Montaigne*, ed. Gide (New York: McGraw-Hill, 1959), p. 24.
23. Gide, "Concerning Influence in Literature," trans. Blanche A. Price, in *Pretexts*, ed. Justin O'Brien (New York: Meridian, 1959), p. 37.
24. Franz Kafka, *The Diaries of Franz Kafka*, trans. Joseph Kresh, ed. Max Brod (London: Schocken, 1948), II, 228.

The absurdist's agonizing sense of isolation evokes repeated justifications and blasphemies in the face of a deaf society (more bored than surprised) and of the eternal silence of the infinite spaces. The novel's humanism has not been cajoled into pinning its faith on man's reason, reasonableness, or predictability. The underground man blames utopian humanists for assuming consistency in man, but he is driven mad by his unbearable sense of the inconsistency of individual lives. "You want to cure man," says Dostoevsky's absurdist to his humanist, "of his bad old habits and reshape his will according to the requirements of science and common sense. But what makes you think that man either can or should be changed in this way?" [25] Montaigne would ask the same question of his social philosophers (and much the same of the absurdist). Man is "patchwork and motley," and his trajectory is a "drunkard's motion, staggering, dizzy, wobbling" (pp. 511, 736). He is constantly prey to the treachery of his own nature. In how many ways does Montaigne claim, as the underground man does, that "men love abstract reasoning and neat systematization so much they think nothing of distorting the truth," or that "a man might go insane on purpose, just to be immune from reason"? [26]

Montaigne does not have to go insane on purpose, for he does not seek the truth. The philosopher who can endure pain patiently is quite antipodal to the nineteenth-century intellectual whose toothache is "strident and perverse." [27] Montaigne's humanism makes of tolerance a mode of moral evaluation as the absurdist makes of suffering a moral transvaluation. While Montaigne inductively philosophizes the self, the anguish of situation is cooled by domestic detail. The absurdist temperament is an instance of a psychologizing that becomes common by refusing to be general.

Even *in extremis* Montaigne will not credit himself with being the noblest sufferer of them all:

25. Dostoevsky, *Notes from Underground*, p. 116.
26. *Ibid.*, p. 107.
27. *Ibid.*, p. 100.

Democritus and Heraclitus were two philosophers, of whom the first, finding the condition of man vain and ridiculous, never went out in public but with a mocking and laughing face; whereas Heraclitus, having pity and compassion on this same condition of ours, wore a face perpetually sad, and eyes filled with tears. . . . I prefer the first humor, not because it is pleasanter to laugh than to weep, but because it is more disdainful, and condemns us more than the other; and it seems to me that we can never be despised as much as we deserve. Pity and commiseration are mingled with some esteem for the thing we pity; the things we laugh at we consider worthless. I do not think there is as much unhappiness in us as vanity, nor as much malice as stupidity. We are not so full of evil as of inanity; we are not as wretched as we are worthless (pp. 200–1).

The humanist admits weaknesses and terrors because they are universal; he does not admire them because they are imagined to be unique. *We* replaces the *you* or *I* of the absurdist. Montaigne expects less of mankind than does the absurdist, so he accepts more. The absurdist's moral revulsion (a sentiment foreign to Montaigne) is symptomatic of an apocalyptic impatience for total change, a hope for innocence and salvation, for a new age. It is what George Eliot calls the "mistaking [of] indignation for virtue." [28] Montaigne is not interested in the morality of a human situation, but rather in the humanness of a moral question. He stands behind the epiphany of Italo Svevo's confessor, Zeno: "Life is neither good nor bad; it is original." [29] Sensing that to be absolutely right is to be more or less than human, the humanist cannot be a prosecutor.

If we look again at Montaigne's evaluation of Democritus and Heraclitus, we note that vanity, stupidity, and inanity are moralized by the absurdist into unhappiness, malice, and evil. Inevitably, he uses literature as exorcism, setting up his characters as targets. Dostoevsky's confessor says at the end of his account, "I've felt ashamed all the time I've been writing this story, so it isn't litera-

28. George Eliot, "The Morality of Wilhelm Meister," in *Essays*, p. 147.
29. *The Confessions of Zeno* will be discussed in Chapter Five.

13

ture, but a punishment and an expiation." [30] Seeking no scapegoat, Montaigne's centrifugal generosity is based on his deep faith in the continuing folly of mankind and his abiding trust that man's limitations cannot be surpassed. He has been, in Nietzsche's words, "cured . . . of taking history too seriously." [31]

Sainte-Beuve's caricature of Montaigne's temperament unwittingly reveals the way in which Montaigne's humor relieves his despair:

> His playfulness and casualness are purely superficial. Montaigne . . . is a kind of sorcerer, an evil genius who takes us by the hand, and who, guiding us through the labyrinth of opinion, tells us at every step, just when we think we know where we stand, "All this is false, or at least dubious; don't give your trust so readily. . . ." The world is to be grasped as a great, gloomy, endless universe moving silent and unknown under skies perpetually gray. . . . Montaigne's charm and good humor serve merely to screen off the spectacle of the abyss or, as he would put it, to prettify the tomb.[32]

But Sainte-Beuve undervalues Montaigne's playfulness. Rather than prettifying the tomb, it helps us to live in front of it.

Because he is not overwhelmed by the farce of history, the humanist does not seek to escape the abyss by crawling into it. The absurdist, pretending to dismiss history utterly, is the one who takes it seriously; allegorizing it, he finds relief in seeing his generation as a "great aggregation of fools." The humanist neither reduces nor aggrandizes by adjusting history. For him, the psychology of progress or that of regression is self-indulgence.

With many others who assume humanism's dependence on tradition, Jaspers ardently seeks a perspective that would link era to era:

> A widening chasm between us all and previous history makes this a general, fundamental question of our life: how can a part

30. Dostoevsky, *Notes from Underground,* p. 202.
31. Nietzsche, "Thoughts out of Season," in *Philosophy,* p. 223.
32. Sainte-Beuve, "Montaigne," p. 25.

of the irretrievable past, something we can neither bring forward nor continue, be ours in memory and indeed serve us as space, then as yardstick, and finally as moving impulse? How can we receive it not in dogmatic traditionalism, not in relativistic indifference, not in aesthetic irresponsible emotion, but as a claim upon us, affecting all that we are.[33]

Jaspers' focus reflects the famous divisions—between fathers and sons, God and Christ, God and his world, politics and religion, aristocrats and the people—that are played with in the nineteenth-century Russian novel. The concentration is on the fissures between generations rather than on the humanist's connecting bridge of man's character. One of the major points in this book is that the absurdist, able to come to terms with the present only by transcending or humiliating it, perpetuates the splits between ages, as between the world and himself, his authorship and his characters, his art and his life. He emphasizes historical differentiation in order to resist his own times, thereby excusing his own sense of exile. He finds havens of refuge in the past and the future.

The humanist has a more relaxed attitude. The present, for him, parallels most periods of human existence, though the forms of tension and the texture of different eras may vary. He expresses the sentiment:

> I hope we are well out of that phase in which the most philosophic view of the past was held to be a smiling survey of human folly, and when the wisest man was supposed to be one who could sympathize with no age but the age to come.[34]

For the humanist, history is relevant only as it serves the present consciousness; in his novels, he uses history—either the traditional past or current atmosphere—as the raw material from which to refine the constants in the human situation. He is not afraid of being devoured by the present any more than he is convinced

---

33. Karl Jaspers, *Existentialism and Humanism*, trans. E. B. Ashton (New York: R. F. Moore, 1952), p. 60.
34. George Eliot to Sara Hennell, July 12, 1861, *The George Eliot Letters*, ed. Gordon S. Haight (New Haven: Yale Univ. Press, 1955), III, 437.

that his novel can swallow up his sense of the world's absurdity.

Montaigne's rejection of miracle and eccentricity is a rejection of the magic of history's remoteness and of literature as ritual. It is a recommendation of the ever contemporary game of "gay and sociable wisdom" between author and reader (p. 857). Montaigne's relation to his work and its sources, which predicts the relation of author to character in novels like those of Austen, George Eliot, and James, is endorsed by Gide's famous exposure of the paradox of classicism. Rousseau boasted: "I know my own heart and understand my fellow man. But I am like no one in the whole world. I may be no better, but at least I am different." The classicist, rising to the commonplace, makes good Rousseau's boast:

> The wonderful thing is that [the classicist] thus becomes more personal. But he who flees humanity for himself alone, succeeds only in becoming special, bizarre, incomplete.[35]

Montaigne says: "I must go the same way with my pen as with my feet" (p. 758). But Flaubert writes: "The principal thing in this world is to keep one's soul aloft, high above the bourgeois and democratic slough. The worship of art gives one pride: no one can have enough of it. Such is my morality."[36] The path from the aesthetic pinnacle to the underground man's mousehole is clear.

The problems of the humanist novelist are related to the accelerating popularity of the absurdist's habit of castigating his age through forms of confession and parody that isolate consciousness from common relations. To be heard, the humanist must increasingly make conversation out of confession, dialogue out of monologue, for he seeks, as ever, to make man whole out of fragmented parts. Hamlet, crawling between heaven and earth, and poor forked Lear on the heath have invaded the novel's stage, and the

35. Gide, "Concerning Influence," p. 31.
36. Flaubert to Laure de Maupassant, Feb. 23, 1873, *The Selected Letters of Flaubert*, ed. and trans. Francis Steegmuller (New York: Farrar, Straus & Cudahy, 1953), p. 246.

humanist must somehow put them to work. He does so by refusing to drop the curtain. He too is tempted to annihilate personality by ennobling, brutalizing, or dissolving it, but he will not stay with sainthood or blasphemy, choose murder or insanity. George Eliot, Forster, and Camus may find temporary relief in the nonhuman, in escape from the world of "petty jealousies and unrest," but they go back.[37] They use retreats to avoid transcendence, not the world. The Dostoevsky who, in his diaries, prosecutes, hates, and vilifies in the name of love, and who, in *Notes from Underground*, lacerates and abuses his idealism, is tried as the tragic paralytic Ivan Karamazov and is released on bond to Alyosha. His probationary characters are prodded from private uniqueness to public eccentricity, from expectation of the commonplace to the miraculous, from love in the marketplace to dreams, but the resulting novel transfigures and turns back the fantastic journey as it tames the "savageries" of fanaticism.[38]

The absurdist direction deliberately leads life away from literature so that literature may become the novelist's history. Flaubert's scorn for democratic alliances between himself, his characters, and his audience is antipodal both to "that pact of generosity between author and reader," which Sartre sees as the essential fictional relation,[39] and to the intention of the George Eliot who writes:

> Art is the nearest thing to life; it is a mode of amplifying experience and extending our contact with our fellow-man beyond the bounds of our personal lot. All the more sacred is the task of the artist when he undertakes to paint the life of the People.[40]

37. George Eliot to Bessie Rayner Parkes, July 15, 1852, *Letters*, II, 45.
38. In his introduction to Dostoevsky's *Winter Notes*, Saul Bellow writes: "In the novel the writer cannot permit himself to be sour, jaundiced, cruel, intemperate and arbitrary. There savageries are tamed by truth" (p. 26).
39. Sartre, *What Is Literature?*, trans. Bernard Frechtman (New York: Philosophical Library, 1949), pp. 54–55.
40. George Eliot, "The Natural History of German Life," in *Essays*, p. 271.

No one knew better than Flaubert how to draw George Eliot's "peasant in all his coarse apathy, and the artisan in all his suspicious selfishness," but at best a condescending pity replaces the sympathy George Eliot calls for.[41] The artist clearly does not seek identity: "As for me," writes Flaubert, "I fail to understand how these people live who are not from morning to night in an aesthetic state." [42] A clear difference emerges between Flaubert's exclusive nature and Forster's humanist attitude, in which art supports life instead of seeking to conquer it:

> Art is not enough, any more than love is enough, and thought isn't stronger than artillery packs now, whatever it may have been in the days of Carlyle. But art, love and thought can all do something, and art, the most nervous of the three, mustn't be brushed aside like a butterfly. . . . It has become part of our armor.[43]

Forster's "armor" protects the human from the nonhuman, not the artist from his subjects. We are reminded that humanism is a defensive posture and that, as Forster puts it, tolerance has always had a bad press. The acceptance of the partial and the approximate means the unpalatable acceptance of impermanent and imperfect relationships in the present. Flaubert refuses that compromise when he writes: "I thought [love] was something independent of everything, even of the person who inspired it. When two persons love, they love for ten years without seeing each other, without suffering any ill effects therefrom." [44] His dictionary of bourgeois commonplaces is an ironic antithesis to the epigraphs at the head of George Eliot's chapters. While Flaubert rails against the necessity of living in the alien skins of his characters and resents being part of mankind, George Eliot asserts:

41. *Ibid.*
42. Flaubert to Louise Colet, Oct. 3, 1846, *Letters*, p. 83.
43. Forster, "A Note on the Way," in *Abinger Harvest* (London: Edward Arnold, 1953), p. 89.
44. Flaubert to Louise Colet, 1848, *Letters*, p. 93.

If the human race has a bad reputation, I perceive that I cannot escape being compromised. And thus, while I carry in myself the key to other men's experience, it is only by observing others that I can so far correct my self-ignorance.[45]

The two professions are emblematically contrasted in anecdotes of Kierkegaard and James. Kierkegaard's vivid description of the unheeded apocalyptic clown suggests the absurdist's separation of writer from reader in terms of trust and tone:

It happened that a fire broke out backstage in a theater. The clown came out to inform the public. They thought it was a jest and applauded. He repeated his warning, they shouted even louder. So I think the world will come to an end amid general applause from all the wits, who believe that it is a joke.[46]

James gives us a counterimage of communication, the humanist's turning of apocalypse into a recognition of shared endurance. As a boy he witnessed a farcical theatrical entertainment. The audience was tense with concern because a certain ship sailing from America to Europe was overdue. Mr. Mouser jumped about the stage, pursued by a troupe of laundresses, but when the curtain fell he appeared at the footlights, still in his costume of farce, and announced breathlessly, "Ladies and gentlemen, I rejoice to be able to tell you that the good ship Atlantic is safe." James describes the reaction:

The house broke into such plaudits, so huge and prolonged a roar of relief, as I had never heard the like of and which gave me my first measure of a great immediate public emotion— even as the incident itself today reminds me of the family-party smallness of the old New York, those happy limits that could make us all care, and care to fond vociferation, for the same thing at once.[47]

45. George Eliot, *The Impressions of Theophrastus Such* (New York: Harper, 1902), p. 8.
46. Kierkegaard, *Either/Or*, I, 24.
47. Henry James, *Autobiography*, ed. Frederick Dupee (New York: Criterion, 1956), pp. 157–58.

It is not a question of bad news and good news. If we extrapolate the two scenes, we may imagine that the apocalyptic clown had trained his audience to a competitive wit, not to a reflective humor. The "humanist" audience is able to distinguish art from life and to hear news from both worlds.

Still, for me the capital difficulty remains style, form, that indefinable Beauty implicit in the conception and representing, as Plato said, the splendor of Truth.

That is when we should have lived.

Gustave Flaubert

CHAPTER TWO

Sentimental Education:
The Absurdist Novel as History

WHEN BALZAC announces in his introduction to *Etudes de Moeurs* that it is not enough to be a man—one must be a system, we are not convinced by his arrogant dehumanization, by this drive toward synthetic purity. His well-advertised search for the absolute is always mocked by his absorption in life and in the life of his novels, and he can never relinquish his delight in what James calls the "sense of another explored, assumed, assimilated identity." But Flaubert's imagination is never overcome by the dreams and acts of his characters, and his deliberate vision leads us away from the novels to his own agonizing and isolated drama of creation. Flaubert writes in a tone of mock humility of his detachment from his peers, his public, and their politics:

> I shall spend my life gazing at the Ocean of Art, while on it others navigate or do battle; and from time to time I shall entertain myself by plunging to the bottom in search of bright-hued shells that no one will want. I shall keep them for myself alone, and use them to cover the walls of my hut.[1]

1. Flaubert to Louise Colet, Oct. 7, 1846, *The Selected Letters of Flaubert,* ed. and trans. Francis Steegmuller (New York: Farrar, Straus & Giroux, 1953), p. 85.

This diver for the "pure Idea," this hutted "brahmin" who seeks the pitch of perfection, is so overcome by the recognition which the humanist uses as a starting point, "the vanity of ourselves, of our plans, of our happiness, of beauty, of goodness, of everything," that he particularizes it as his martyrdom.[2] His bourgeois novels, recoiling from a world with no progress or purpose, refuse to come to terms with it. A society impeccably mocked by its own rhetoric is meant to remind us that its personality and politics are farce. With no resources in the present, experience is relentless, not educative. The "mandarin"[3] desperately seeks to engineer an escape from his mortal dress through the scapegoat skins of his problematic characters.[4] He seeks a path from the middle ground of moral education to a myth of permanence in the land of romance. The saving fiction is the past:

> Have you sometimes thought what it must have been like, the night of a triumph—the legions returning, the perfumes burning around the chariot of the conqueror, and the captive kings marching behind? And the circus! That is when we should have lived: then it was possible to breathe, and breathe a true poetic air, whole lungfuls of it, as on a mountaintop, until the heart pounded![5]

No atmosphere could be more alien to the humanist's novel. It became the lyric "half" of Flaubert's fiction, in which even cruelty could be innocent.

To relieve the aversion he feels for his bourgeois characters, Flaubert takes "flights of metaphysics and mythology," and to solace himself for the "poor, scrofulous, fainting century" into which he was born, he converts its process to history, so that

---

2. Flaubert to Maxime du Camp, Apr. 7, 1846, *ibid.*, p. 42.
3. Flaubert reserves this term for himself and a chosen few. For example, see Flaubert to George Sand, Oct. 30, 1870, *ibid.*, p. 235.
4. In a letter to Louise Colet, Flaubert speaks of "having constantly to be in the skins of people for whom [I] feel aversion" (Apr. 6, 1853, *ibid.*, p. 151).
5. Flaubert to Maxime du Camp, Apr., 1846, *ibid.*, p. 44.

bourgeois lives and monarchies might become primitive society warred upon by the kingdom of Art.[6] If art must take place in time, it can at least possess that time. The artist rescues himself from the democratic irony that links him and his characters by making himself, in a fit of transvaluation, a version of "the People . . . the tradition of Humanity."[7] As the novel dooms his characters to a common mortality, waste, and flux, it becomes for the novelist exorcism and escape, scalpel and wand. Solitude is the inevitable fate and privilege for the man who makes of the understanding that "sorrow comes from attachment" a motivation for withdrawal.[8] Flaubert's lament "The earth is no longer habitable for us poor mandarins" can be quieted only by a kind of moral suicide, what Nietzsche, speaking of Flaubert, calls "the will to nonentity." It is a claim for innocence, a retreat from relationship to style.

Nietzsche's specific criticism of the superhistorical man applies to Flaubert, to his "loathings and . . . wisdom." The philosopher pleads for an abandonment of the protective ordering of antiquity, and his words apply to all devices of preservation by abstraction. He is, of course, concerned with attitudes toward the sense of history; we cannot escape history but must not overvalue it:

> The value we put on the historical may be merely a Western prejudice; let us at least go forward within this prejudice and not stand still. If we could only learn better to study history as a means to life! We would gladly grant the superhistorical people their superior wisdom, so long as we are sure of having more life than they. . . . By excess of history, life becomes maimed

6. Flaubert to Louise Colet, Apr. 6, 1853, *ibid.*, p. 151; and Flaubert to Ernest Feydeau, Jan. 11, 1859, *ibid.*, p. 200.

7. Flaubert to George Sand, May 10, 1867, *ibid.*, p. 211.

8. The full comment is a citation from Sakiya-Muni, which Flaubert reproduces with approval: "He who has understood that sorrow comes from attachment retires into solitude like a rhinoceros" (Flaubert to Maxime du Camp, Apr., 1846, *ibid.*, p. 44).

and degenerate, and is followed by the degeneration of history as well.[9]

Visions can educate and transform experience into possibility. But when they are meant to grant us the consolations of permanence and compensation for change, they do not serve life. Flaubert's mind feeds on an apocalypse of history in the past and that of art in the future; he thereby starves his characters. He admits:

> In our appetite for life we feast again on past feelings and dream of the future. Bound to the present, the soul is stifled; the world is not big enough for it.[10]

The dreams of Flaubert's trapped bourgeois souls are pale and ironic reflections of his self-serving imagination, sterile domestic fantasies that close doors to education and escape. Unfortunately, the world *is* big enough for those souls. James's protest against Flaubert's separation of authorial imagination from its natural sympathies and extensions in character is a decidedly moral one:

> Singular enough in his life the situation so constituted: the comparatively meagre human consciousness—for we must come back to that in him—struggling with the absolutely large artistic.[11]

But Flaubert insists on the moral superiority of his absolutely large artistic consciousness. Dwelling among his dreams, he escapes from the ethical confinements of this world to gain a moral victory over life:

> At times I have feelings of great despair and emptiness—doubts that taunt me at my moments of naïvest satisfaction. And yet I would not exchange all this for anything, because my con-

9. Nietzsche, "Thoughts out of Season," in *The Philosophy of Nietzsche*, trans. Oscar Levy, ed. Geoffrey Clive (New York: New American Library, 1965), p. 224.

10. Flaubert to Louise Colet, Aug. 15, 1846, *Letters*, p. 71.

11. Henry James, "Gustave Flaubert," in *Notes on Novelists* (New York: Scribner's, 1914), p. 95.

science tells me that I am fulfilling my duty, obeying a decree of fate—that I am doing what is Good, that I am in the Right.[12]

Such a rationalization would be severely mocked within his novel, bound as it is to the rack of small rounds and spans.

Flaubert relieves the endless and daily labor of living with his characters by visions of anarchy more bacchicly manic than any Nietzschean "joy in unwisdom":

> The human soul is at present sleeping, drunk with the words it has heard; but some day it will awake in a frenzy and give itself over to an orgy of Freedom; for there will no longer be anything to restrain it, neither government, nor religion, nor any formula.[13]

There is little charity in this picture and much moralizing, for its fervid design of fantasy corrects the present without making demands on personal responsibilities. The hope is for escape from the delusions by which we must live, but the paradise is not peopled by Flaubertian characters. The orgiastic awakening to freedom follows an apocalyptic destruction explicitly voiced in Flaubert's early notebooks:

> I wouldn't mind a bit seeing all civilization crumble like a mason's scaffolding before the building was finished—too bad! . . . I'd enjoy being at the gates of Paris with five hundred thousand barbarians, and burning the whole city. What flames! What a ruin of ruins! [14]

This kind of pronouncement helps to ward off fears of a "democratic" anarchy like that described in Sentimental Education, in which the mob destroys the Palais Royal. It also reveals the phantasmagoric heights of Flaubert's hopes, the perfectionism of his expectations. But the image is most helpful in effecting

12. Flaubert to Louise Colet, Apr. 24, 1852, Letters, p. 133.
13. Flaubert to Louise Colet, Sept. 4, 1852, ibid., p. 141.
14. Flaubert, Intimate Notebook, 1840–41, trans. Francis Steegmuller (New York: Doubleday, 1967), p. 19.

his desired separation from those who must practice the contemporary game. This position is apparent in his famous claim (and what a claim for literature!), after the wreck of the Tuileries in 1870, that "this would never have happened if they had only understood *L'Education sentimentale.*"[15] The picture of ruin summoned up by the young Flaubert makes an interesting contrast to that of civilized creation actually seen by James's young Hyacinth Robinson at a time when the hero of *The Princess Casamassima* is obliged to contribute to the destruction of inherited orders. Hyacinth's bewildered consciousness is tortuously checked by the visible evidence of civilization's accomplished beauty. Torn by the tension between the cause of civilization's people and the art of its masters, what he feels denied by his politics is precisely what he feels expressed in the history of art, "a sense of everything that might hold one to the world."[16] His suicide paradoxically affirms the value of his world. Flaubert would prefer to let his world commit suicide so that he would not have to struggle continuously for the style that would disengage him from it. At his projected scenes of holocaust, Flaubert is seated apart from the mankind that "disavows" him, a voyeur of ruin.[17] He yearns to be superfluous to the needs of the time. Such is his resentment of days that are not romance, of the novel that is not poetry.

Flaubert prefaces his "orgy of Freedom" vision with a criticism of social utopianism that is remarkably similar in tone and substance to that of Dostoevsky's underground man. Although Flaubert recognizes the necessity for suffering and the inevitability of imperfection, his aesthetic dreams of a state "superior to life itself" strangely resemble those of the political Ivan Karamazov, who for all his differences, not the least of which is his

---

15. This remark, often cited, appears in Harry Levin, *The Gates of Horn* (New York: Oxford Univ. Press, 1966), p. 288, and the accompanying footnote traces it to Maxime du Camp, *Souvenirs littéraires* (1883), II, 474.
16. James, *The Princess Casamassima* (New York: Harper & Row, 1959), p. 332.
17. Flaubert to Louise Colet, Apr. 24, 1852, *Letters*, p. 133.

fiction, touches Flaubert's case.[18] Both cynical hermits of idealism ardently desire to escape from the uncertain and unjust present by demanding historical orders in which the lion will lie down with the lamb. Both use history to reject the contemporary world on the grounds that it is absurd. Flaubert crumbles formulas by an explosive projection of anarchy and thinks he is overpowering absurd systems, but in fact he is only consoling himself with a time-worn obsession: "I keep seeking—without ever finding—that idea which is supposed to be the foundation of everything." [19] It is the outrageous logic that Ivan insists upon, and it is safe, because both know the physical present can never overcome a metaphysical idea. Flaubert's dream of the future's release from bourgeois morality reaches back over the present to a reconstructed tyranny of the past, invulnerable to both moral education and evaluation. The middle ground of morality resists permanence. But unfettered from this place, a man may escape its hundred daily deaths.

Lukács convincingly attributes the "decorative and exotic" nature of Flaubert's romanticism to its function as a counterimage to the "hated and despised prose of every day bourgeois life."[20] He blames Flaubert's loss of contact with the people for sapping the novel's energy and truth. Less polemical readers of Flaubert's bourgeois novels would tend rather to resent the author's separation of sympathies from his characters in order that the past can only devaluate the present. When James speaks of Frédéric's bankruptcy as a hero, he contends that "it is somehow the business of a protagonist to prevent in his designer an excessive

18. *Ibid.* Dostoevsky's famous diatribes against socialism and Catholicism may be profitably compared to those of Flaubert. In addition to his remarks in *Notes from Underground*, ed. and trans. Ralph Matlaw (New York: E. P. Dutton, 1960), key arguments are to be found in *Winter Notes on Summer Impressions*, trans. R. L. Renfield (New York: McGraw-Hill, 1965), p. 115, and in *Diary of a Writer*, ed. and trans. Boris Brasol (New York: Scribner's, 1949).

19. Flaubert to George Sand, Dec. 20, 1875, *Letters*, p. 251.

20. Georg Lukács, *The Historical Novel*, trans. Hannah and Stanley Mitchell (Boston: Beacon, 1962), p. 206.

waste of faith." [21] Flaubert's artistic faith brilliantly accomplishes what it sets out to do, but the protagonist requires of it much more than Flaubert is prepared to give.

Sentimental Education spares the reader the need for extended sympathy. The art of the novel is not here a marriage of minds, but rather that of the saint and his sanctity, and the novel is loved with a love "exclusive, ardent, devoted." [22] Such devotion makes a religious place of the work of fiction, now an instrument of salvation for its maker. Better than any life that can be lived in the present or that it can depict, the novel describes only to overcome, reflects only to compensate. The Flaubert who "digs and burrows into the truth as deeply as he can, who likes to treat a humble fact as respectfully as a big one, who would like to make you feel almost *physically* the things he reproduces," [23] is working to cure himself of the imperfect love of mortals. In answer to Louise Colet's question "Do you love me?" he gives an unconsoling yes:

> If you grant that it is possible to be in love and yet realize how immensely pitiful are the rewards of love as compared with the rewards of art, and feel an amused and bitter scorn for everything that drags you down to earth;—if you admit that it is possible to be in love and yet feel that a line of Theocritus is more intoxicating than your most precious memories, and feel too that you are quite willing to make big sacrifices (I mean of the things generally considered the most precious: life, money) whereas you would refuse to make small compromises.[24]

Flaubert's aesthetic historicism affords him an illusion he can live by: the nostalgic dream of artists, as "they once existed,"

> whose loves and minds were the blind instruments of the appetite for the Beautiful, God's organs by means of which He demonstrated to Himself His own existence. For them the

---

21. James, "Flaubert," pp. 82–83.
22. Flaubert to Louise Colet, Aug. 9, 1846, *Letters*, p. 63.
23. Flaubert to Louise Colet, Jan. 16, 1852, *ibid.*, p. 127.
24. Flaubert to Louise Colet, late Apr., 1847, *ibid.*, pp. 86–87.

world did not exist; no one has ever known anything of their sufferings; each night they lay down in sadness, and they looked at human life with astonished gaze, as we contemplate ant-hills.[25]

Elevated above and shielded from the world by style, the artist would be like the Zeus who can be philosophic because he is amoral. It is a vision that dwarfs into ridiculous pathos the energy to begin anew of both characters and readers. The artist achieves a kind of immortality of which his characters are incapable, and he gains it at their expense. (Proust accomplishes a similar salvation, but not before his characters give him analogies which, with his own experience as Marcel, educate him to a transcendence so bold that it turns escape into a victorious vision, a pitch Flaubert was never to reach.) Flaubert desperately needs a balm for the perishing and the changing: "In my soul I have already attended a thousand funerals; my friends leave me one after the other, they marry, move away, change."[26] His fear of the temporal closes the windows of his fiction's house: "I have long since come to realize that in order to live in peace one must live alone and seal one's windows lest the air of the world seep in."[27]

Flaubert's painful and deliberate selection of words wards off the possibility of being taken by surprise, of having another's choice and direction catch him off guard. He thoroughly knows his characters and just how far they can go from the beginning, and the reader is not allowed the illusion that those characters might ambush their author. Art saves him from the commitments of love and relationship. He hides in that vague place "where no one loves me or knows me, where my name means nothing to anyone, where my death or my absence costs no one a tear."[28]

25. Flaubert to Louise Colet, Aug. 9, 1846, *ibid.*, p. 63.
26. *Ibid.*, p. 66.
27. Flaubert to Louise Colet, Sept. 18, 1846, *ibid.*, p. 76.
28. Flaubert to Louise Colet, Aug. 9, 1846, *ibid.*, p. 65. The places of prostitution afford the same hiding place, and Flaubert's obsessive linking of the ascetic with the voluptuous has often been noted. For an excellent analysis of the uses and meanings of prostitution in Flaubert's work, see the chapter on *Sentimental Education* in Victor Brombert, *The Novels of Flaubert*

When he accuses Louise Colet of loving him too much, he is demanding that she relieve him from loving. The novel helps him to detach himself, and its characters help him to retire from the human comedy.

The search for permanence, which determines Flaubert's form and tone, is centrally illustrated in the Fontainebleau scene of *Sentimental Education*. The retreat from political Paris to fabled Fontainebleau by Rosanette and Frédéric is a playing out of the tension between the contemporary and the historical. As usual, because the characters cannot hold much pressure, the contest is exteriorized. The tentative relationship in the foreground is surrounded by reminders of idyllic, unchanging forms in peace. All process has been put to rest, and life is muralled on successive walls of art and nature. The "lingering splendour" of Diane de Poitiers in the guise of the mythical Diana fills Frédéric with "an indescribable feeling of retrospective lust." [29] Flaubert is at once criticizing Frédéric's paralysis, the contemporary relationship, and the arbitrary connections between external stimuli and moods which we consider authentic and self-generated. His letters and his "romantic" novels are evidence of Flaubert's own retrospective lust for the finished passion. He gives an unusually profuse and detailed description of the day's scenery, which serves as a dwelling place for this passion. Then he enters the novel formally:

> Royal residences have a melancholy all their own, which is probably due to the disproportion between their immensity and the tiny number of inhabitants, to their silence, which seems surprising after so many fanfares have been sounded there, and to their unchanging luxury, which proves by its antiquity the

(Princeton: Princeton Univ. Press, 1966). Many critics have noted Flaubert's compulsive identification of lust and death in the spending of the self. See Levin, *Gates of Horn*, p. 242; Brombert, *Flaubert*, p. 288; and Jean-Pierre Richard, "The Creation of Form in Flaubert," trans. Raymond Giraud, in *Flaubert: A Collection of Critical Essays*, ed. Giraud (Englewood Cliffs, N.J.: Prentice-Hall, 1964).

29. Flaubert, *Sentimental Education*, trans. Robert Baldick (Baltimore: Penguin, 1964), p. 320. Future references will be to this edition and will be noted in the text.

transience of dynasties, the inevitable impermanence of all things; and this emanation of the past, as overpowering and funereal as the scent of a mummy, affects even the simplest mind (pp. 320–21).

The act of seeing the nonhuman relieves Flaubert from the passion that becomes prostitution in the merely human world:

> At times I look on animals and even trees with a tenderness that amounts to a feeling of affinity; I derive almost voluptuous sensations from the mere act of seeing—when I see clearly.[30]

For the artist, seeing clearly is an act of eternal love; but for Frédéric, seeing has to decline into living. Rosanette's yawn, the reaction of "even the simplest mind" to this deathly splendor, sends the characters back to their days and nights, while Flaubert stays behind to outlast their transience. Only the dead can defeat death, and Rosanette's merely human needs doom her to mortality. After his sister's funeral, Flaubert gives the dead their due: "More intelligent than any of us, certainly, were the stones, which had understood it all long ago and perhaps still retained something of its meaning."[31] Only history can compensate for the tedium of time in process, for its torture. And since he delights in contrasting the beauty of ancient tyrannies with the stupidity of modern democracy, Flaubert annihilates Rosanette's yawn with nostalgia:

> The road zigzagged between dwarf pines under rocks with rugged outlines; all this part of the forest had something muffled, quiet, and solitary about it. It conjured up thoughts of the hermits of old, the companions of the great stags with fiery crosses between their horns, who used to receive with fatherly smiles the good kings of France as they knelt in front of their grottoes. The warm air was full of the smell of resin; tree-roots interlaced on the ground like veins. Rosanette stumbled over them, felt miserable, and wanted to cry (p. 321).

30. Flaubert to Alfred le Poittevin, May 26, 1845, *Letters*, p. 36.
31. Flaubert to Maxime du Camp, Apr. 7, 1846, *ibid.*, p. 42.

Again he has crushed a contemporary scene with one that once existed. Immortal ichor flows in the veins of the past. The veins of the present dry up in the corpse of Rosanette's baby. Flaubert is on the scene, seeing clearly. Careful to avoid authorial guilt by association (very different from personal exorcism by identification—"Madame Bovary, c'est moi"), he inserts himself as a silent and undramatic witness whose mute eyes set Rosanette's small selfishness in perspective:

> A painter in a blue smock was working at the foot of an oak, with his paint-box on his knees. He looked up and watched them pass (p. 321).

The artist, like nature, "more intelligent than any of us," has been fully educated to see in the spirit of justice, not of grace.[32] He watches the scene condemn itself in passing.

Rumors of the confused political turmoil filter through the woods from Paris, but that battle, like the relationship, is mocked by the forest's metaphors of giantism and magic, cathedral and apocalypse: "bore themselves like patriarchs or emperors"; "symmetrical as organ-pipes"; "like a group of Titans"; "thoughts of volcanoes, floods, great unknown cataclysms"; "they had been there since the beginning of the world and would stay like that until its end" (p. 323). For Rosanette, who lives for the day, apocalypse is maddening. For Frédéric, as for Flaubert, such spans are comfort for the rough, petty imperfections of the present. But only for a while can Fontainebleau draw the vanishing present into its spellbinding remembrance of things past, covering it with the illusion of immortality. Frédéric feels certain "that he [will] be happy for the rest of his days" (p. 325). With this sentence, Flaubert pushes his hero away from him. What follows is a patronizing punishment for those who dream of immortality

32. The notion of justice and science as ideal measures of political and aesthetic worth is a common theme in Flaubert's letters. The terms appear together in a letter to George Sand, Apr. 29, 1871, *ibid.*, p. 237. See also Flaubert to George Sand, June–July, 1869, *ibid.*, p. 220; and Flaubert to Mlle Leroyer de Chantepie, Mar. 18, 1857, *ibid.*, p. 195.

in the world of sensation. This is the most typical of Flaubertian tones and the one farthest removed from the ironic sympathy of moral extension which is George Eliot's; it depends on an excoriating reduction of the best experience to clichés of non-dimensional repetition and a diminution of possibility and choice to indifference. Gestures and words, dictionaries of banalities in the hands and mouths of his dreamers, save Flaubert from the shame of being taken in by life:

> They would lie face to face in the grass, gazing deep into each other's eyes, slaking the constant thirst they had for one another, and then remaining silent with half-closed eyelids. . . .
> "Why, of course! It's the insurrection!" Frédéric would say with a disdainful pity, for all that excitement struck him as trivial in comparison with their love and eternal Nature (p. 325).

When we see eternal nature silently mocking their love, history deriding their story, Flaubert's impassivity taunting their pity, we can understand why Rosanette feels she is getting old at twenty-nine. Even the tragic recital of her life is diminished by cold summary and Frédéric's clichéd sympathy: "How you've suffered, my poor love" (p. 327). Flaubert comes directly into the scene after an exchange of half-truths between the lovers with the assurance that "complete relationships are few and far between" (p. 328). The one we have in front of us is demoted to the general pile of ruins by the sentence "The poor Marshal had never known a better one" (p. 328). The humanist never questions that "complete relationships are few and far between," but he survives his disappointments without resorting to preventive medicines of satire. Clearly Flaubert's intention is not that of the humanist. On the surface it may seem that Frédéric is sacrificing his interest in the mystery of Rosanette's personality and past for the melodrama of Paris. Actually he is running away from the recognition that he already knows her too well. And Flaubert is doing the same thing. Instead of setting up educative contrasts of dimension and significance, the alternation between private and public worlds reveals a fearful fact: because we and Flaubert can completely fix the personalities the novelist sets before us and the world he describes, we must be pushed on by chance and fate like Frédéric, since we are not motivated by psychological curiosity. The reader is determined. Much of his interest and attention is directed to little enigmas and puzzles in the plot, allusions, half-hidden scenes and secret societies, and crafty movements of symbolic objects from one house to another. Frédéric is moved to Paris because it is there and not here, because he hopes to find himself a history superior to personality.

But the political scene, pushed into the foreground because it is being lived in the present, is no more tolerable than the personal scene. Flaubert historicizes them both. Public experience bares its clichés even more evidently than private experience: "Honor to our fallen heroes" (p. 332). Flaubert flattens moral subtleties by converting character to history:

> By and large the National Guards were merciless. . . . Despite their victory, equality—as if to punish its defenders and ridicule its enemies—asserted itself triumphantly: an equality of brute beasts, a common level of bloody atrocities; for the fanaticism of the rich counter-balanced the frenzy of the poor, the aristocracy shared the fury of the rabble, and the cotton nightcap was just as savage as the red bonnet (p. 334).

He lets equality prosecute, but the moralizing that is usually filtered through overheard rhetoric is here exposed. He himself is a victim of romanticizing and cliché-making as soon as he betrays his disappointed expectations:

> Now property was raised to the level of Religion and became indistinguishable from God. The attacks being made on it took on the appearance of sacrilege, almost of cannibalism. In spite of the most humanitarian legislation ever passed in France, the spectre of '93 reappeared, and the sound of the guillotine made itself heard in every syllable of the word "Republic"—although this did not prevent people from despising it for its weakness. Conscious of no longer having a master, France began to cry

out in terror, like a blind man without a stick, or a child who has lost its nurse (p. 295).

He must separate himself from Frédéric's drifting drama of repetition. His lofty demands cannot but make a myth of failure, an allegory of disappointment. His indignation turns naturally to crude satire when M. Roque takes to his bed, after he has murdered, with the complaint that he is too sensitive for revolutions (p. 336). Flaubert's tone is the melodrama of murdered progress.

M. Roque is brutally caricatured, but we are not convinced that greater spirits than his are somewhere to be found, whose presence could console us for our regressions. Flaubert denies us the service of his own spirit and furnishes us, instead, names from history; typically, they humiliate us by their retrospective stature:

> It was customary for every person in the public eye to model himself on some famous figure, one copying Saint-Just, another Danton, and yet another Marat (p. 301).

There can be only one victory in Flaubert's novel: its creation. Life's clichés cannot be defeated within the novel, only by it. Flaubert gets into the lifeboat of art, while his characters flounder in wave after wave of unshaded coordinates, stylistic equivalents of endlessly repetitive sentimental educations: "Frédéric thought about his room at home, about the plot of a play, about subjects for pictures, about future loves" (p. 16). His novel describes the category generation over the category individuality.[33] The rhythm of the times is the rhythm of character. The humanist clearly distinguishes the public from the private tempo. He sides with Nietzsche's belief that "history, as far as it serves life, serves an unhistorical power."[34] For the humanist, history is the servant of life, not its master, and is obliged to submit to an unpredictable present.

33. These terms are used by Kierkegaard in *The Present Age*, trans. Alexander Dru and Walter Lowrie (London: Oxford Univ. Press, 1949), p. 28. Frédéric's occasional privilege of objective judgment is token, since it never succeeds in distinguishing him.
34. Nietzsche, "Thoughts out of Season," p. 224.

Behind an easel at Fontainebleau, Flaubert can compensate himself for the passing of the human scene with the permanence of its reproduction. He resents the notion that fiction must entertain because the prose of democracy subjects art to decay, and he considers the artist to be fortunately cursed with the affliction of "a special language." [35] This is hardly to be shared, since his words must divide him from a vulgar history. The burden of writing "a well-composed description that will please as many bourgeois as possible" only spoils the purity of his experience.[36] We remember Flaubert's self-portrait as the ocean-gazer who adorns his private walls with his bright shells. The business of his art is to preserve its creator from the death that squeezes his characters. If the novelist's characters are so thoroughly exposed by their language that everyone can understand them, their creator gains a hidden sanctuary behind them. Poor Frédéric has only the clichés of the unconditional and the absurd dreams of the conditional in which to find permanence:

> Now and then she smiled, and her eyes rested on him for a moment. Then he felt her gaze penetrating his soul, like those great rays of sunlight which go down to the depths of the water. He loved her without any reservation, without any hope of return, unconditionally; and in those mute transports, which were like bursts of gratitude, he would have liked to cover her forehead with a rain of kisses (p. 93).

Since relationship inevitably changes, to be kept inviolate it must be fantasized:

> And they imagined a life which would have been entirely devoted to love, rich enough to fill the widest deserts, surpassing all joys, and defining all sorrows; a life in which the hours

35. Flaubert to Louise Colet, 1846, *Correspondance* (Paris, 1926–33), I, 239 (my translation). The sentence reads: "J'ai l'infirmité d'être né avec une langue spéciale dont seul j'ai la clef." For an interesting and penetrating discussion of Flaubert's anguishing suspicion of even the artist's words as a mode of salvation, see Leo Bersani, "Flaubert: The Politics of Mystical Realism," *Massachusetts Review* (Winter, 1970), pp. 35–50.
36. Flaubert to Maxime du Camp, April, 1846, *Letters*, pp. 43–44.

would have gone by in a continuous exchange of confidences;
a life which would have become something splendid and sublime like the shimmering of the stars (p. 271).

To pay for this fantasy, which Flaubert finds in his own soul, his
characters must suffer it as their only reality. Flaubert devotes
himself to its description, and thereby strives to go beyond it,
since the uncommitted word will not decay like love. Unlike art,
love speaks in a style indistinguishable from a thousand others:

> Their tastes and opinions were identical. Often the one who
> was listening would exclaim:
> "So do I!"
> Then there would follow endless complaints about Fate:
> "Why didn't heaven allow it? If only we had met. . . ."
> "Ah, if I had been younger!" she would sigh.
> "No! if I had been a little older!" (p. 271).

We can admire the precision of Flaubert's summation, and we
might imagine that this is the way he gets his vengeance on the
bourgeois reader who spoils his solitary reveries, forcing him to
escape by writing "a well-composed description."

The lovers, denied style, have only the allegory of fate to keep
experience uncontaminated. The "generous" competition to
equalize their ages must remain a conditional game to prevent a
fearful realization. The same vocabulary of love's clichés serves,
at the end of the novel, to excuse the self from life's failures.
Deslauriers and Frédéric "blamed chance, circumstances, the
times into which they were born" (p. 418). Next to these stabs
at historical martyrdom, Flaubert's look noble indeed, and this
may account for the feeling of James, D. H. Lawrence, and
others that the most moving tragedy in Flaubert derives from the
disproportion between his sensibility and that of his characters.
But because Flaubert forces his characters to live *for* him, at times
their pathos, as in the final scene between Mme Arnoux and
Frédéric, makes us impatient with Flaubert's personal complaints.
At least we mildly pity their inability to retreat from life to a
higher vision. Their creator can relieve himself by saying:

I am turning toward a kind of aesthetic mysticism . . . and I wish it were stronger. When you are given no encouragement by others, when you are disgusted, frustrated, corrupted, and brutalized by the outside world, so-called decent and sensitive people are forced to seek somewhere within themselves a more suitable place to live.[37]

Poor Frédéric cannot do much with the times into which he was born, certainly not elevate his fate out of it by historicizing his martyrdom into an apocalyptic warning and justification like Flaubert's: "If society continues on its present path I think we shall see a return of such mystics as have existed in all the dark ages of the world." [38] As Flaubert withdraws he leaves behind pale parodies of his dreams, his disappointments, and his protective patterns, trapped in the consciousness of Frédéric.

Frédéric's love, like Flaubert's, is best when he is mentally or physically absent. Then it takes on a "sort of funereal sweetness, a sleepy charm" (p. 105). In these self-sealing adjectives, we recognize the attraction of the past at Fontainebleau, the sensuous inertia of retrospective lust. This is quite different from the deaths in life, which spring upon us and oppress us with the sense of our decomposition. At Rosanette's party, Frédéric glimpses a world of death in the midst of life, and his description sounds very much like those in Flaubert's letters: "Whole worlds of misery and despair, a charcoal stove beside a trestle-bed, and the corpses at the mortuary in their leather aprons, with the cold tap-water running over their hair" (pp. 130–31). We are relieved when Frédéric's fear of the aged Mme Arnoux offering herself to him leads to an empty distraction and this tired comment: "In every parting there comes a moment when the beloved is already no longer with us" (p. 415). The vision of the mortuary, comparable to the actual death of the baby, mocks the funereal comfort of the dreams of both Frédéric and Flaubert, just as life in the provinces before his inheritance mocks Frédéric's late pastoral

37. Flaubert to Louise Colet, Sept. 4, 1852, Letters, pp. 140–41.
38. Ibid.

dream of "the peace of the country, a sleepy life among simple-hearted folk, in the shadow of the house where he was born" (p. 409). Like all Frédéric's projections, this is motivated by reaction, not insight. And the death of M. Dambreuse, celebrated by aborted clichés, is not different from any death we can imagine in the novel:

> All the speakers took the opportunity to thunder against So-cialism, of which Monsieur Dambreuse had died a victim. It was the spectacle of anarchy together with his devotion to law and order, which had cut short his days. They extolled his in-telligence, his probity, his generosity, and even his silence as a deputy, for, if he was no orator, he was endowed with those compensatory virtues which were infinitely preferable, and so on and so forth. . . .
> The pebbly earth fell into place; and the world had done with Monsieur Dambreuse (p. 377).

The attempted elevation of personality to history is a mockery; history within the novel cannot make us more permanent than love.

In his attack on historicism, Lévi-Strauss writes:

> All meaning is answerable to a lesser meaning, which gives it its highest meaning, and if this regression finally ends in recog-nizing a contingent law of which one can say only: *it is thus*, and not otherwise, this prospect is not alarming to those whose thought is not tormented by transcendence even in a latent form.[39]

Flaubert's cool surface appears to tell us exactly that it is thus. But the regression that Lévi-Strauss recommends describes only the humanist's path. Flaubert, suffering from the truth, tormented by the need for transcendence, does not take this road. As a novel-ist, he seeks a consoling form, but his characters want a consoling attitude. For the humanist, the lesser meaning that gives reality to

39. Claude Lévi-Strauss, *The Savage Mind* (Chicago: Univ. of Chicago Press, 1966), p. 255.

the higher is character. When Frédéric tries to distract himself from his passion, he attempts at one point to write a history of the Renaissance. Flaubert allows him a temporary balm and comments, "He forgot his own personality by immersing it in that of others—which is perhaps the only way to avoid suffering from it" (p. 188). The authorial intrusion is revealing; it points to a process of identification almost entirely opposite to that of the humanist's negative capability, in which the authorial self is included in the novel's educative play. Frédéric, like Flaubert, finds in history not example but escape, and one much more meager than that of his creator. Escape into history is escape from personality. We are left with death in life. Flaubert's need to escape from the alien skins he forms is what makes Lukács call him "one of the most important precursors of dehumanization in modern literature." [40] The discovery that art must substitute for an unbearable present puts him in the line of fiction's absurdists.

40. Lukács, *Historical Novel*, pp. 194–95. James makes a similar accusation in his essay on Flaubert in *Essays in London and Elsewhere* (London: J. R. Osgood, McIlvaine & Co., 1893), p. 158, as does Jean-Paul Sartre in his projected study of Flaubert in *Search for a Method*, trans. Hazel E. Barnes (New York: Knopf, 1963).

. . . being just now bound to tell a story of life at a stage when. . .

I am rather weighed down with anxiety now . . . and find life, even in the middle of my many blessings, still a difficult and sometimes a toilsome journey. I have always to struggle against a selfish longing for repose.

George Eliot

CHAPTER THREE

Daniel Deronda:
The Humanist's Ironic Presence

W HEN FLAUBERT seeks to escape self-irony through an ironic dissection of others, his presence is nevertheless dramatically felt; the reader is continuously aware of a suffering and self-lacerating imagination that is superior to what it describes. To be at her best, George Eliot must project self-irony from within the novel. She depends on this projection, which provides the major link between character, author, and reader, for her primary tone and intention. The irony of self tempers the irony of others, and the novelist's critical humor pretends to a mutual education, surprised and teased at every turn.[1] It is because we have this illusion in the Gwendolen part of *Daniel Deronda* that we feel so disappointed by its absence in the Jewish half, in which George Eliot allows herself to be absorbed by the "divine Unity" of

---

1. George Eliot writes, "It is only by observing others that I can so far correct my self-ignorance as to arrive at the certainty that I am liable to commit myself unawares" (*The Impressions of Theophrastus Such* [New York: Harper, 1902], p. 8). Flaubert and George Eliot have often been contrasted, especially on the basis of their diametrically opposed narrative techniques. Robert Scholes and Robert Kellogg discuss the validity of this contrast in *The Nature of Narrative* (New York: Oxford Univ. Press, 1966), pp. 197–98.

Daniel, Mirah, and the spirit of Mordecai.[2] When prophecy over-comes the tension between vision and act and replaces the humor that endures it, the novel's story becomes a romance of history.[3] As George Eliot historicizes herself, Gwendolen, left behind, should become emblematic of the fate of a selfish and secular England. But Gwendolen resists George Eliot's participation in her own betrayal. The expansion of personality into history seems to humiliate Gwendolen's world, yet Zionism is embarrassed by Gwendolen's small personal vow, "I will try" (p. 340). George Eliot's own large vision is possible only through Gwendolen's unwitting generosity. Henry James, speaking through his character Constantius, says:

> [Gwendolen's] finding Deronda pre-engaged to go to the East and stir up the race-feeling of the Jews strikes me as a wonderfully happy invention. The irony of the situation, for poor Gwendolen, is almost grotesque, and it makes one wonder whether the whole heavy structure of the Jewish question in the story was not built up by the author for the express purpose of giving its proper force to this particular stroke.[4]

No one can doubt the necessity of Deronda's vision for Gwendolen's drama. James implies as well that Gwendolen, rather than George Eliot, has the last word, for it is only by her conscience and its growth into "helpless maturity" that the Jewish question can be tolerated.

This effect, in which a larger vision is in the service of a humbler one, in which history serves life instead of shaping it, is central to the humanist's novel. With this direction it is impossi-

2. For the suggestive analogy, see George Eliot, *Daniel Deronda* (New York: Harper, 1960), p. 612. Future references will be to this edition and will be noted in the text.

3. The betrayal of the Gwendolen half by the Jewish half has been assumed by almost every critic of *Daniel Deronda* and has often been analyzed as a wish fulfillment disguised in the robes of fiction. See F. R. Leavis, *The Great Tradition* (New York: Doubleday, 1954), pp. 103-4. See also note 11 below.

4. Henry James, "*Daniel Deronda*: A Conversation," in *Partial Portraits* (London: Macmillan, 1905), p. 90.

ble for the novelist to abandon his characters to epoch and cause with impunity. If such a novelist is tempted to try to rise without irony above story, on the wings of philosophy, it is the responsibility of his most vital character to show up the cheat. He pays dearly for raising the pitch of art beyond the range of dramatic conscience, for "conquering" his fiction.

When George Eliot has dissolved the tension between what we can see and what we can do, we are in the presence of revelation:

> The world seemed getting larger round poor Gwendolen, and she more solitary and helpless in the midst. The thought that [Deronda] might come back after going to the East, sank before the bewildering vision of these wide-stretching purposes in which she felt herself reduced to a mere speck. There comes a terrible moment to many souls when the great movements of the world, the larger destinies of mankind, which have lain aloof in newspapers and other neglected reading, enter like an earthquake into their own lives—when the slow urgency of growing generations turns into the tread of an invading army or the dire clash of civil war, and grey fathers know nothing to seek for but the corpses of their blooming sons, and girls forget all vanity to make lint and bandages which may serve for the shattered limbs of their betrothed husbands. Then it is as if the Invisible Power that has been the object of lip-worship and lip-resignation became visible, according to the imagery of the Hebrew poet, making the flames his chariot and riding on the wings of the wind, till the mountains smoke and the plains shudder under the rolling, fiery visitation. Often the good cause seems to lie prostrate under the thunder of unrelenting force, the martyrs live reviled, they die, and no angel is seen holding forth the crown and the palm branch. Then it is that the submission of the soul to the Highest is tested, and even in the eyes of frivolity life looks out from the human scene of human struggle with the awful face of duty, and a religion shows itself which is something else than a private consolation (pp. 606–7).

We can compare this expansion, by which George Eliot escapes Gwendolen's side and leaves her bound, with the kind of dra-

matic intensity by which the novelist's humor and sense of proportion link her closely to Gwendolen. After ringing Gwendolen
with the world's woes, George Eliot asks early in the novel:

> What in the midst of that mighty drama are girls and their blind
> visions? They are the Yea or Nay of that good for which men
> are enduring and fighting. In these delicate vessels is borne on-
> ward through the ages the treasure of human affections (p. 90).

We may flinch at the elevated rhetoric, but a deliberate disproportion sets up a critical and saving perspective. Inevitably,
George Eliot is questioning the possibility of reflecting the larger
universe in an affection that can be felt only in a smaller one.
The moment that George Eliot makes her own artistic success
problematic by raising the question of the novel's range, she
takes her place next to a limited Gwendolen, and the reader finds
his own restricted measure. The humanist is at his best when he
cannot get off the ground.

In the first of these citations the invisible is made visible and
therefore actual, as Deronda and George Eliot carry Mordecai's
prophetic vision to a promised land. The epigraph to chapter 53
insinuates that Deronda, the sturdy vessel of the Hebrew spirit,
is, like Moses, an artist by right of historical inheritance. This is
indeed compensation for his missed musical career and for the unhappy life of his mother. But the property of art, George Eliot
reminds us at the beginning of chapter 23, is not inherited. It is
earned by hard fighting.[5] The contest between property and art,
which runs all through the novel and is overcome in the marriage
of Miss Arrowpoint and Klesmer, is crucial to the difference between Gwendolen's fate and Deronda's destiny. Gwendolen's bit
of earth will have to be fought for, that poor earth bound by the
range of human affections. Deronda's mission is bequeathed, and
vague references to a difficult future cannot convince us as much
as Gwendolen's tears or George Eliot's irony. Prophecy has

---

5. See the first epigraph to chapter 23. This is one of the most persistently
pursued themes in the novel.

given both Deronda and his novelist a possessory title to life's meaning; their sympathy for Gwendolen, who will have to struggle for an "ungotten estate" (p. 186), is therefore both posed and patronizing.

In her tableaued march toward Zionism, George Eliot is victim of a perspective that is blurred and romanticized by distance, even though she has recognized the dangers inherent in the use of perspective as the central metaphor in the novel's moral and aesthetic structure:

> It is to be believed that attendance at the *opéra bouffe* in the present day would not leave men's minds entirely without shock, if the manners observed there with some applause were suddenly to start up in their own families. Perspective, as its inventor remarked, is a beautiful thing. What horrors of damp huts, where human beings languish, may not become picturesque through aerial distance! What hymning of cancerous vices may we not languish over as sublimest art in the safe remoteness of a strange language and artificial phrase! (p. 114).

While the final operatic drowning, a reality that completes the gothic melodrama of warning faces merely "started up" in Gwendolen's own family, is a chillingly effective and ironic stripping of the artifice of distancing, George Eliot's attempt to realize Deronda's vision by comparing his life with alien lives fails. Stereotyping the Jew as the Cohen family and romanticizing him through the historical cliché of Mordecai's prophetic vision deaden Deronda instead of vivifying him. George Eliot subverts her two great thematic tensions—the contested claims of outside and inside and those of the universal and the particular—which have compromised the novelist's powers as much as her heroine's. The novelist, she reminds us flippantly, did not create perspective and can only manipulate it. But through Mordecai and Deronda she invents horizons instead of stumbling upon them and relaxes the strain of being merely human.

The expansion of personal fate into historical destiny dissolves paradox, as the Cohen family, embodying and exteriorizing the most common ethnic clichés, drains vulgarity from Mordecai,

Deronda, and Mirah—the "best selves" of a spiritualized culture. The Jewish future, carried by its "frail incorporation of the national consciousness,"[6] will not be subject to the same waves that rock Gwendolen's frail vessel. The whole of Mordecai's poverty is blessed by consolations of historical fulfillment. His environment serves his vision, and his personality is freed from the burden of ordinary human affections. He falls in love with Deronda because of Deronda's history. And George Eliot does too, though not without apology:

> To say that Deronda was romantic would be to misrepresent him; but under his calm and somewhat self-repressed exterior there was a fervour which made him easily find poetry and romance among the events of everyday life. And perhaps poetry and romance are as plentiful as ever in the world except for those phlegmatic natures who I suspect would in any age have regarded them as a dull form of erroneous thinking. . . . How should all the apparatus of heaven and earth, from the farthest firmament to the tender bosom of the mother who nourished us, make poetry for a mind that has no movements of awe and tenderness, no sense of fellowship which thrills from the near to the distant, and back again from the distant to the near? (p. 151).

Deronda eludes the tragic clash of perspectives because, once George Eliot gives him "all the apparatus of heaven and earth," he escapes from the "near," merely brushing it in his talks with Gwendolen and the Cohen family. When George Eliot asserts that "we keep a repugnance to rheumatism and other painful

6. See p. 388, where this phrase is used to describe Mordecai's life. The metaphor of incorporation is a constant one whenever George Eliot deals with the larger and selfless universe of history and philosophy in relation to the individual will. The metaphor is given an ideological base in this chapter ("Revelations"), but it is a major design in the novel, from the first reference to double perspective in Klesmer's discussions of art and in Deronda's dreams. For a good discussion of the relation of this chapter to Matthew Arnold's theological essays, see U. C. Knoepflmacher, *Religious Humanism in the Victorian Novel* (Princeton: Princeton Univ. Press, 1965), pp. 62–63.

effects when presented in our personal experience" (p. 114), we are prepared for Gwendolen's eventual shock. How fully Grandcourt dramatizes the fall into the particular. But when Deronda's dreams project him to the "quest of a beautiful maiden's relatives in Cordova, elbowed by Jews in the time of Ibn-Gebirol" (p. 284), we are not prepared for the horror of a Jewish reality. The Cohen family allows Deronda's dream to continue and finally to be realized. The climactic wedding is freed from care by their noisy presence:

> So when the bridal veil was around Mirah it hid no doubtful tremors—only a thrill of awe at the acceptance of a great gift which required great uses. And the velvet canopy never covered a more goodly bride and bridegroom, to whom their people might more wisely wish offspring; more truthful lips never touched the sacramental marriage-wine; the marriage blessing never gathered stronger promise of fulfillment than in the integrity of their mutual pledge. Naturally, they were married according to the Jewish rite. And since no religion seems yet to have demanded that when we make a feast we should invite only the highest rank of our acquaintance, few, it is to be hoped, will be offended to learn that among the guests at Deronda's little wedding-feast was the entire Cohen family, with the one exception of the baby who carried on her teething intelligently at home. How could Mordecai have borne that those friends of his adversity should have been shut from rejoicing in common with him? . . . Jacob ate beyond his years; and contributed several small whinnying laughs as a free accompaniment of his father's speech, not irreverently, but from a lively sense that his family was distinguishing itself (pp. 610–11).

When destiny is a gift and art and spirit are inherited property, North and South, East and West, old and new, Christ and Moses, the ends of the earth and history can embrace, freed from the encumbrances of the grotesque and the particular. The Cohen family's compensatory vulgarity is too cumbersome to be convincing, much less to make the purity of the spiritual trinity convincing.[7] George Eliot's sense of perspective is left at home teething with the baby, while the Cohen family saves Mordecai from one cliché and allows him to assume another:

> Ezra Cohen was not clad in the sublime pathos of the martyr, and his taste for money-getting seemed to be favoured with that success which has been the most exasperating difference in the greed of Jews during all the ages of their dispersion. This Jeshurun of a pawnbroker was not a symbol of the great Jewish tragedy; and yet was there not something typical in the fact that a life like Mordecai's . . . was nested in the self-gratulating ignorant prosperity of the Cohens? (p. 388).

Was ever a family so used by history? We are unmoved by this artifice of balance. George Eliot must emphasize the sympathies of Deronda and Mordecai because she fears they are too pure to be felt. Her contrast of the poets Young and Cowper can be applied to her own characters:

> The sum of our comparison is this—In Young we have the type of that deficient human sympathy, that impiety towards the present and the visible, which flies for its motives, its sanctities, and its religion, to the remote, the vague, and the unknown: in Cowper we have the type of that genuine love which cherishes things in proportion to their nearness, and feels its reverence grow in proportion to the intimacy of its knowledge.[8]

Like Young, Deronda leaves the fireside for "Virtue sitting on a mount serene." [9] Because his conscience "included sensibilities beyond the common, enlarged by his early habit of thinking himself imaginatively into the experience of others" (p. 384), he has license to insist that Mordecai sympathizes with the near:

> "I don't think you will find that Mordecai obtrudes any preaching. . . . He is not what I should call fanatical. I call a man

7. Similarly, the Meyricks are too naïve to be convincing; they merely set off Mirah's natural intelligence and sensitivity and proclaim Deronda's goodness.
8. George Eliot, "Worldliness and Other-Worldliness in the Poet Young," in *Essays of George Eliot*, ed. Thomas Pinney (New York: Columbia Univ. Press, 1963), p. 385.
9. *Ibid.*, p. 371.

fanatical when his enthusiasm is narrow and hoodwinked, so that he has no sense of proportions, and becomes unjust and unsympathetic to men who are out of his own track. Mordecai is an enthusiast" (p. 427).

If we are not convinced by this picture of Mordecai's intellectual tolerance, George Eliot adds this testimonial:

> Mordecai's brilliant eyes, sunken in their large sockets, dwelt on the scene with the cherishing benignancy of a spirit already lifted into an aloofness which nullified only selfish requirements and left sympathy alive. But continually, after his gaze had been travelling around on the others, it returned to dwell on Deronda with a fresh gleam of trusting affection (p. 611).

We are left out of this closed circle of admiration.

In one of her conversations with Deronda, who set up affection as the highest good, Gwendolen muses, "I should have thought you cared most about ideas, knowledge, wisdom and all that" (p. 312). We hope, like Gwendolen, to be convinced of his genuine sympathy for the near. Instead, Deronda justifies himself without measuring the needs of Gwendolen:

> "But to care about *them* is a sort of affection. . . . Call it attachment, interest, willingness to bear a great deal for the sake of being with them and saving them from injury. Of course it makes a difference if the objects of interest are human beings; but generally in all deep affections the objects are a mixture— half persons and half ideas—sentiments and affections flow in together" (p. 312).

Gwendolen answers with flirtatious naïveté and affection that allow her to apply this definition to herself:

> "I wonder whether I understand that. . . . I believe I am not very affectionate; perhaps you mean to tell me, that is the reason why I don't see much good in life" (p. 312).

Humor and perception raise her above the moralistic Deronda. She charms us back into the circle of feeling . We are involved in

Gwendolen's displays of spite, in her rejections of clichéd roles of virtue. She says of Mirah: "I have no sympathy with women who are always doing right. I don't believe in their great sufferings" (p. 329). While George Eliot has her speak for all who are jealous of those who have inherited their destinies, the novelist exorcises her fears that the reader will feel the same way about Mirah.

One of the most interesting indications of change in direction is pointedly exhibited in the epigraph to chapter 20. Apology and justification rush into George Eliot's tone:

> It will hardly be denied that even in this frail and corrupted world, we sometimes meet persons who, in their very mien and aspect, as well as in the whole habit of life, manifest such a signature and stamp of virtue, as to make our judgment of them a matter of intuition rather than the result of continued examination.[10]

The epigraph calls our attention to the significant contrast between Gwendolen and Mirah. For all her weeping, Mirah encounters no real obstacles to keep her from a great future. The first words of the epigraph deliberately narrow our area of doubt. Again and again in the Jewish half, the novel's original question, "Was she beautiful or not beautiful?" is replaced by "Was there not something typical in the fact?" (p. 388). The first part of the novel is continually punctuated with the doubt "Who can all at once describe a human being?" (p. 79), and Gwendolen's story forces George Eliot to explore the question in depth. Mirah and Mordecai must be known all at once since they are not known at all, but Gwendolen's development from mastery to bewilderment is impressive. Ironically, in a description of Gwendolen's limited vision, George Eliot grants her a humanity superior to Deronda's:

> And Gwendolen?—she was thinking of Deronda much more than he was thinking of her—often wondering what were his

10. George Eliot's identification reads, "Alexander Knox: quoted in Southey's Life of Wesley."

54

ideas "about things," and how his life was occupied. But a lap-dog would be necessarily at a loss in framing to itself the motives and adventures of doghood at large; and it was as far from Gwendolen's conception that Deronda's life could be determined by the historical destiny of the Jews, as that he could rise into the air on a brazen horse, and so vanish from her horizon in the form of a twinkling star (p. 411).

We are tempted to echo Nietzsche: "We would gladly grant the superhistorical people their superior wisdom, so long as we are sure of having more life than they." [11]

Deronda's privileged access to others has nothing to do with life:

> Our consciences are not all of the same pattern, an inner de-liverance of fixed laws: they are the voice of sensibilities as various as our memories (which also have their kinship and likeness). And Deronda's conscience included sensibilities be-yond the common, enlarged by his early habit of thinking him-self imaginatively into the experience of others (p. 384).

This feeble romance of the soul bypasses the difficulty of know-ing others and invites George Eliot's artistic surrender. In the

---

11. Nietzsche, "Thoughts out of Season," in *The Philosophy of Nietzsche,* trans. Oscar Levy, ed. Geoffrey Clive (New York: New American Library, 1965), p. 224. The question of George Eliot's impulsion toward idealization has been intelligently examined in: Knoepflmacher, *Victorian Novel,* pp. 255–56; Jerome Thale, *The Novels of George Eliot* (New Haven: Yale Univ. Press, 1959), p. 77; and Quentin Anderson, "George Eliot in *Middle-march,*" in *From Dickens to Hardy* (Baltimore: Penguin, 1958). George Levine, asking why characters like Mordecai and Deronda are failures, astutely hypothesizes: "Their kind of heroism was what she aspired to, but it was also incompatible with her particular vision; it suggested the possibility of great and rapid changes, of significant and conscious tamper-ing with the course of history, where, as a determinist, she instinctively felt that such tampering had become almost impossible" ("Determinism and Responsibility in the Works of George Eliot," in *A Century of George Eliot Criticism,* ed. Gordon S. Haight [New Haven: Yale Univ. Press, 1954], pp. 352–53). Levine's article is particularly relevant to my focus be-cause it concentrates on the positive force that derives from an essentially negative perspective. As Thale puts it: "The minimal quality of her faith seems to give it special validity. . . . She believes in so little we feel there is justification for what she does believe" (*George Eliot,* p. 19).

first scene of chapter 17, just before Deronda is to see Mirah as "the impersonation of misery" (p. 139), George Eliot describes Deronda's passage from seraphic boyhood to worthy promise:

> [He is] not seraphic any longer: thoroughly terrestrial and manly; but still of a kind to raise belief in a human dignity which can afford to acknowledge poor relations (p. 138).

The cunning metaphor of generosity painlessly becomes his story. And nothing is more instructive than the difference between the ambivalence of Gwendolen's emotions and the certainty of Deronda's. A nature "liable to difficulty and struggle" (p. 240) never materializes; it can only be defined outside of itself, since George Eliot has allowed us no room to go inward, no space between skin and soul. Deronda and Mirah are all they appear to be and only that. In the process of purification, George Eliot elevates Deronda's celebrated sympathies to a level of allegory that kills them for the reader—to "a resentment on behalf of the Hagars and Ishmaels of the world" (p. 326). Ironically, the birth of "historic sympathy" (p. 271) is supposed to achieve for him a sense of reality that his diffuse compassion has denied him. The discovery of Deronda's history can only be recapitulated as plot. It allows him to skip over the purgatory of individual conscience, which has been exchanged for tradition. Daniel's makings of "Pericles or Washington" (p. 128) are almost the unmaking of the novel. (Deronda often seems like a background figure in the standard historical novel who has been moved awkwardly up front where the small fictional players are meant to perform.) Fortunately, his presence does work for Gwendolen's story.

The problems of knowing and seeing are eased for Mirah too. Because the unholy ghost that scares Gwendolen at Offendene and haunts her wedding projects from Gwendolen's fear of herself, it can never be captured (p. 340). But since Mirah's faces from the past are all external to herself, they come into being and can be conquered. Her fears are soothed by the sense that they are essentially historical and privileged ones, the makings of a great destiny. She contradicts Mrs. Meyrick's hopes of assimilation by reciting a past she pretends to fear: "I will always cling to my people. I will always worship with them" (p. 280). How detached this is from Gwendolen's disinherited cry: "Ah, poor mamma! . . . Don't be unhappy. I shall live. I shall be better" (p. 609).

Mordecai's self-fulfilling vision mutes the novelist's voice. His own magic and full knowledge "spontaneously plant him on some spot where he [has] a far-stretching scene" (p. 356); because he is superhistorical, he sees beyond our horizon. What role can the novelist have here? Where is the dramatic voice that defends and criticizes in the same breath, that involves us in the process of knowing? Where is the voice that says of Gwendolen:

> Perhaps if Klesmer had seen more of her in this unconscious kind of acting, instead of when she was trying to be theatrical, he might have rated her chance higher (p. 234).

This humanist voice ends Gwendolen's story with the question "How am I to begin?" (p. 411). And it takes us back to the novel's first epigraph, which gently mocks the human need for the sense of beginnings and endings by raising to the level of drama the "all-presupposing fact with which our story sets out." The gambling scene is a fine picture of that assumption; the novelist is making her facts seem like chance, and her character is trying to make of chance a direction. This dual action functions in the finest parts of the novel. The necessary impression of constantly renewed beginnings, both aesthetic and moral, ends when George Eliot sails toward the one true beginning. Then both novel and hero are sanctified by an act that goes beyond them. George Eliot inherits the kingdom of Art.

Throughout the first part of the novel an unassimilated voice reminds us of the difference between the novel's material and psychological density and the abstractions of an idealized world, the one that resists large philosophic consolations and the other that forges them. Philosophy makes its way in a very real world:

Contemptible details these, to make part of a history; yet the turn of most lives is hardly to be accounted for without them. They are continually entering with cumulative force into a mood until it gets the mass and momentum of a theory or a motive. Even philosophy is not quite free from such determining influences; and to be dropt solitary at an ugly irrelevant-looking spot with a sense of no income on the mind, might well prompt a man to discouraging speculation on the origin of things and the reason of a world where a subtle thinker found himself so badly off (p. 169).

That Mordecai would not think of such a connection shows us how far removed he is from George Eliot as novelist.[12] For she herself is clearly indicating that the novelist's dream is just as hampered by necessities as is Gwendolen's. It is only by surrendering her task to Deronda and Mordecai that George Eliot frees herself from a mortal vocabulary. They launch the novel from "the wide sky, the far-reaching vista of bridges, the tender and fluctuating lights on the water which seems to breathe with a new life that can shiver and mourn, be comforted and rejoice" (p. 361). The words of the psalmist give her the repose she longs for but usually knows she must struggle against. Her resistance to this luxury, her submission to contemptible details, marks the novelist of the best parts of *Daniel Deronda*.

George Eliot consistently tests the limits of her own novelistic consciousness as she probes the boundaries of Gwendolen's capacities for judgment:

> But, let it be observed, nothing is here narrated of human nature generally: the history in its present stage concerns only a few people in a corner of Wessex—whose reputation, however, was unimpeached, and who, I am in the proud position of being able to state, were all on visiting terms with persons of rank (p. 66).

12. We get an insight into George Eliot's pattern of idealization by comparing the way in which wealth frees character *for* experience in James's novels with the way in which poverty frees Mordecai *from* experience here.

The pretense of authorial dependence is a familiar humanist game, and by now it may seem too heavy. But the inclusion of self within the confines of social vision is a perspective that opens every window to the reader. The novelist plays at complaint, but there is no question of withholding her sympathy. She is a decidedly moved mover, even when she takes the role of traditional puppeteer:

> I am not concerned to tell of the food that was eaten in that green refectory, or even to dwell on the glories of the forest scenery that spread themselves out beyond the level front of the hollow; being just now bound to tell a story of life at a stage when the blissful beauty of earth and sky entered only by narrow and oblique inlets into the consciousness, which was busy with a small social drama almost as little penetrated by a feeling of wider relations as if it had been a puppet-show (p. 109).

The reminder works, though it may sound mechanical, because we are forced to ask: Whose consciousness? George Eliot checks her wisdom to stay near Gwendolen.

It is only when she is absorbed by Deronda that her dramatic cooperation vanishes. When Deronda tells Gwendolen to "take [her] present suffering as a painful letting in of light" (p. 340), his words, unlike those of the novelist, are clearly not intended to sound in a shuttered world. Although George Eliot is convinced of the delusiveness of knowing beyond the affections, beyond what the moral sensibilities can tell us, she allows Deronda to live in a world in which "affections are clad with knowledge" (p. 340) and have a larger dignity of order. When Deronda's world is no longer checked by the novelist feeling her way toward souls, moral pressure, like aesthetic, is relieved; only when this pressure is contained—the world's resistance to being known *a priori*—do we absorb the story. We never feel Deronda's suffering for wisdom; and having felt George Eliot's, we sense the betrayal of our expectations. Deronda petitions for his knowledge, and he receives it full-grown, circumventing the

59

present and pointing him toward the future. Consciousness is inevitably belittled when it does not grow in the present.

George Eliot says of the moral sensibilities of Gwendolen and Grandcourt that "the desire to conquer is a form of subjection" (p. 77). Again she betrays her temptation to punish Gwendolen with a self-righteousness released from the bondage of the novelist's moral humility. The most emphasized contrast between the bonds that insure freedom and the rootlessness that imposes slavery is that between Deronda and Gwendolen. But a more interesting and ironic one, one that is crucial for that tone of tolerance which expands our sympathies, is the contrast between Gwendolen's sense of mastery of personalities and the authorial pose of mystification before the task of knowing the heart. George Eliot restricts our privilege of caricature as she restricts her own:

> Attempts at description are stupid: who can all at once describe a human being? even when he is presented to us we only begin that knowledge of his appearance which must be completed by innumerable impressions under differing circumstances (pp. 79–80).

That George Eliot can so thoroughly *do* Grandcourt in one scene with his dogs does not undo the impression that effort is needed to know the moral sensibilities of men. She warns us about generalizing from a caricatured Mrs. Arrowpoint: "Beware of arriving at conclusions without comparison" (p. 28). Our own checking is George Eliot's way of linking us with her vision and that of her characters. With these constant qualifications, her celebrated patches of philosophy, which structurally appear to be authoritarian, are, like many chapter headings, undergoing criticism by the ensuing drama. Next to George Eliot's reminders, we see Gwendolen's rationalized conclusions. They seem to form the familiar pattern of judgment in process, checked by an open conscience. They carefully reach the positive through the negative. Grandcourt, she muses, "is not ridiculous" (p. 80). But the defensive nature of this exclusive and reductive syllogism immediately exposes it as a caricature of an open mind. She wants to stop at appearances in order to make face value absolute, for it is her face that is her fortune. The insecurity behind this reasoning is sufficiently evident to prevent annihilation of interest in Gwendolen. This reflective play between author and character is heightened by the presentation of Klesmer as patently ridiculous. Gwendolen's initial sense of advantage over him sharpens the inevitable reversal. Because Klesmer himself participates by his judgment and appearance in the rivalry between face and soul, because he suffers in the game before he gains his victory, he succeeds in making himself felt as a critic in a way that Deronda never can. Those who survive the irony of their author are, in the humanist novel, those whom we ultimately honor. Deronda and Mirah too easily profit from their beauty. Gwendolen loses by hers, and Klesmer must make his.

When Gwendolen says that Grandcourt is "adorably quiet and free from absurdities" (p. 100) and that "he never speaks stupidly" (p. 108), we have all we need to measure the counterfeit in Gwendolen's justification of choice. In the beginning she has "a keen sense of absurdity in others" (p. 30); but George Eliot's humor tells us that this sense is really lodged in the novelist, who directs it equally against herself. The description of Gwendolen's poor romance again sets up the contrast between what she can do and not see and what her novelist can see and not do. While the heroine willfully frees herself by romance, she is bound by the economics of need and environment to the slavery of self-justification. George Eliot holds her own vision conspicuously captive, from the beginning, in life's cage:

> She rejoiced to feel herself exceptional; but her horizon was that of the genteel romance where the heroine's soul poured out in her journal is full of vague power, originality, and general rebellion, while her life moves strictly in the sphere of fashion; and if she wanders into a swamp, the pathos lies partly, so to speak, in her having on her satin shoes. Here is a restraint which nature and society have provided on the pursuit of striking adventure; so that a soul burning with a sense of what the

universe is not, and ready to take all existence as fuel, is nevertheless held captive by the ordinary wirework of social forms and does nothing particular (pp. 36–37).

The presence of George Eliot, which insures our involvement in her story, is nowhere more masterfully displayed than when she pretends absence. One of the finest scenes is the early confrontation between Mrs. Arrowpoint and Gwendolen. George Eliot removes herself from the battle to watch, like a god, as her characters go it alone. Two vulnerabilities run for cover while the novelist dramatizes her warnings about easy judgment. With the novelist's protection apparently pulled away, Gwendolen and Mrs. Arrowpoint are both in danger. The scene's humor depends on the presence of its watcher. No one goes uncriticized. Before she exhibits Gwendolen's glib wit, George Eliot describes the limitations of her sensibility:

> It followed in her mind, unreflectingly, that because Mrs. Arrowpoint was ridiculous she was also likely to be wanting in penetration, and she went through her little scenes without suspicion that the various shades of her behaviour were all noted (p. 30).

How thoroughly we are convinced that George Eliot, like us, has made the same mistake. She gives the victim of patronization just enough perception to spoil the victory. The cunning that rejects, separates, and unjustly distinguishes, invites a rain of humor. Gwendolen's confession "I am sure I often laugh in the wrong places" is a rhetorical weapon of wit, an assertion of superiority. The apparently humorless Klesmer resists Gwendolen's easy wit because his criticism is based upon a knowledge of an ironic self, his kindness upon an awareness of the difficulty of earning dignity. Mrs. Arrowpoint must depend on George Eliot to prevent her annihilation; Klesmer does not need her defense, and he profits from her mockery. Because he incorporates the drama of skin against soul and fashion against wisdom, his consciousness has not skipped steps; it lives in the present. And so, we feel, does George Eliot's.

From the beginning of the novel the reader has been conditioned by the sense of continuing and difficult qualification to expect a backlash from any progress. George Eliot says of Mrs. Arrowpoint:

> Several conditions had met in the Lady of Quetcham which to the reasoners in that neighborhood seemed to have an essential connection with each other. It was occasionally recalled that she had been the heiress of a fortune gained by some moist or dry business in the city, in order fully to account for her having a squat figure, a harsh parrot-like voice, and a systematically high head-dress; and since these points made her externally rather ridiculous, it appeared to many only natural that she should have what are called literary tendencies. A little comparison would have shown that all these points are to be found apart; daughters of aldermen being often well-grown and well-featured, pretty women having sometimes harsh or husky voices, and the production of feeble literature being found compatible with the most diverse forms of *physique*, masculine as well as feminine (p. 30).

The fact that Mrs. Arrowpoint has only literary *tendencies* furthers the tease that art is always taken off guard by life and that no advancement in characterization can go unqualified in the novel. Often, in this early part of the novel, the novelist's labor of definition, set deliberately against the rationalized necessity of Gwendolen's, seems forced and self-conscious. When warning us of the difference between Gwendolen's "spiritual dread" and depth of spirit, she writes:

> To her mamma and others her fits of timidity or terror were sufficiently accounted for by her "sensitiveness" or the "excitability of her nature"; but these explanatory phrases required conciliation with much that seemed to be blank indifference or rare self-mastery. Heat is a great agent and a useful word, but considered as a means of explaining the universe it requires extensive knowledge of differences; and as a means of explaining character "sensitiveness" is in much the same predicament (p. 45).

Our constant distraction from attention to story by recall to fine distinctions in terms and feelings, however obtrusive, prepares us for the later tedious backsliding into wisdom that is shared by character, author, and reader. George Eliot reins Rex's moral romance with reminders of the blight of each of life's stages:

> Goodness is a large, often a prospective word; like harvest, which at one stage when we talk of it lies all underground, with an indeterminate future: is the germ prospering in the darkness? at another, it has put forth delicate green blades, and by-and-by the trembling blossoms are ready to be dashed off by an hour of rough wind or rain (p. 48).

Virtue, like art, has no consoling soil. To know would be easier if "greatness [were] dead, and [we could get] rid of the outward man" (p. 74). But the field the novel plows never lies fallow. If Gwendolen cannot marry complacently, neither can George Eliot describe complacently. The consciousness that every appearance may betray its reality is the substance and process of the novel's wisdom.

In a letter to Clifford Albutt, George Eliot defines herself as a conservative who must apologize for the fact that her denials might seem destructive.[13] But the spirit of denial keeps us within the bounds of life. It accompanies the recognition of our "recoverable nature" (p. 525), a nature that prevents Gwendolen's story from becoming history. By these denials we feel the "hidden heroism" (to which we might contrast Mordecai's overt "unapplauded heroism" [p. 409]) of the humanist novel.[14] Hans Meyrick's story of Buddha giving himself to the tigress illustrates the kind of sacrifice the humanist novelist is not willing to make. Personality must remain a problem; it can never be solved by assimilating imperatives which require that "a man die lest he

13. Aug., 1868, *The George Eliot Letters*, ed. Gordon S. Haight (New Haven: Yale Univ. Press, 1955), IV, 472.
14. George Eliot to Mrs. Henry F. Ponsonby, Dec. 10, 1874, *ibid.*, VI, 99.

should spoil his work." [15] The humanist and his novel reject sainthood by turning back from apocalypse to ask over and over again: Was she beautiful or not beautiful?

15. George Eliot to Sara Hennell, Nov. 23, 1864, *ibid.*, IV, 168. This requirement of exalted goodness contrasts with the "everyday serviceable goodness" of George Eliot's stepson Charles.

The human mind is not a dignified organ.

E. M. Forster

But chiefly he talked. As the bottles and bones
Accumulated behind him, the words proceeded
Steadily from the front of his face as he
Advanced into the silence and made it verbal.
Who can tally the tale of his words? A lifetime
Would barely suffice for their repetition;
If you merely printed all his commas the result
Would be a very large volume, and the number of times
He said "thank you" or "very little sugar, please,"
Would stagger the imagination. There were also
Witticisms, platitudes, and statements beginning
"It seems to me" or "As I always say."

Consider the courage in all that, and behold the man
Walking into deep silence, with the ectoplastic
Cartoon's balloon of speech proceeding
Steadily out of the front of his face, the words
Borne along on the breath which is his spirit
Telling the numberless tale of his untold Word
Which makes the world his apple, and forces him to eat.

Howard Nemerov
From "Life Cycle of
Common Man"

CHAPTER FOUR

A Passage to India:
History as Humanist Humor

F LAUBERT'S imagined orgy in which the slumbering spirit of man wakens to an apocalyptic anarchy of sight and sound is a hope never dreamed of in Forster's philosophy. No one knows better than Forster the dictionaries of commonplace that define much of life and the fictions by which we attempt to transcend the prosaic. He muses:

> Most of life is so dull that there is nothing to be said about it, and the books and talk that would describe it as interesting are obliged to exaggerate, in the hope of justifying their own existence. Inside its cocoon of work or social obligation, the human spirit slumbers for the most part, registering the distinction between pleasure and pain, but not nearly as alert as we pretend. There are periods in the most thrilling day during which nothing happens, and though we continue to exclaim, "I do enjoy myself," or, "I am horrified," we are insincere. "As far as I feel anything, it is enjoyment, horror"—it's no more than that really, and a perfectly adjusted organism would be silent.[1]

---

1. Forster, *A Passage to India* (New York: Harcourt, Brace & World, 1924), pp. 132–33. Future references will be to this edition and will be noted in the text.

But because Forster accepts the day that is and views the past as "a series of disorders," he seeks no escape into history, no grounds for an aesthetic martyrdom.[2] That his novel is being written is neither an existential heroic cry against the conspiracy of silence nor a magical act of exorcism. Whatever superiority there is in the order of art consists in its recognition that knowledge is *not* power. Because art is not a history "pressed into shape from outside," it makes the unique claim of being the "only material object in the universe which may possess internal harmony."[3] It is one order of life whose fiction, through its humor, may console us for our inability to remain silent and unjustified.

The novelist is not god, saint, or tortured artist; he is defined like his characters on the wirework of experience and expression, and all the alternatives of perspective and attitude that he cares about and can envisage are contained within the novel. His novel uses occasion; it cannot preserve experience from the attrition of time. By tolerating imperfections of cultures and personalities, the author refuses the nobility of tragedy for the self. Forster's conviction is that the days we live through provide the material to explore spirit. The word cannot release time into space; it is the superhistorical temper that insists on this conversion. Forster humiliates this passion by imagining Godbole's ceremony of spirit, which seems to accomplish this conversion as it is performed and described, from a perspective in which art threatens to become god by seeking a true communion with "the unknown, flinging down science and history in the struggle, yes, beauty herself." Can we determine its final success? he asks:

> Books written afterwards say "Yes." But how, if there is such an event, can it be remembered afterwards? How can it be expressed in anything but itself? Not only from the unbeliever are mysteries hid, but the adept himself cannot retain them. He may think, if he chooses, that he has been with God, but as soon as

2. Forster, "Art for Art's Sake," in *Two Cheers for Democracy* (New York: Harcourt, Brace & Co., 1951), p. 90. One might compare this with the first paragraph on p. 288 of *A Passage to India*.
3. Forster, "Art for Art's Sake," p. 92.

he thinks it, it becomes history, and falls under the rules of time (p. 288).

Forster's history is forever encased in a human mind and contradicts the spatial histories of Flaubert's Fontainebleau and George Eliot's Zionism. He does not lead us, however, to a frustrating nihilism, unless that is where we want to go. The fact that "in time things part" (p. 193) and inevitably we live in time is not a final tragedy. In the exercise of word, spirit, and relationship we learn to live, while still hearing the hundred voices that say, "No, not yet" (p. 322).

The spirit has its moments of unconscious reach, but the novel's order is subject to the same critical forces that assault Ronny's armor and restrict the beauty of Mrs. Moore's escape from tedious responsibilities of judgment and commitment. Forster tests and teases the novel's ability to hold a form while he makes drift out of conversation, relationship, and morality. The dominant rhythm of the novel derives from the frequent passage from overly moral and structured worlds to indifferent, amoral, and amused ones, like the world of nature or of Godbole's ceremony. Again and again Forster flies to the moon to dwarf the world's fictions of habit:

> The game of Patience up in the civil lines went on longer than this. Mrs. Moore continued to murmur "Red ten on a black knave," Miss Quested to assist her, and to intersperse among the intricacies of the play details about the hyena, the engagement, the Maharani of Mudkul, the Bhattacharyas, and the day generally, whose rough desiccated surface acquired as it receded a definite outline, as India itself might, could it be viewed from the moon. Presently the players went to bed, but not before other people had woken up elsewhere, people whose emotions they could not share, and whose existence they ignored (p. 100).

Because Forster's humanism never allows an invulnerable history or nature to destroy or expand his subject permanently, we can take in stride the alarm of a pastoral Camus that "the feeling for history has gradually covered the feeling for nature in the hearts of men, taking from the creator what had belonged to him and giving it to the creature." [4] The humanist novelist challenges abstraction wherever he finds it, especially in varieties of humanism. If nature cannot annihilate men, neither can men control nature. The lordly imperialism of the superhistorical mind, which allegorizes culture and nature to possess them, is overcome by, as often as it re-forms, the exuberant independence of the universe. And the significant contribution of humanist fiction is that it does not choose sides but knows it must live with both. Chapter 10 of *A Passage to India* is a good illustration of Forster's endurance of both nature's indifference and man's compulsion for order. Here he typically undermines the props of his own novel: story and density of character. Following one of the several inconclusive talks between the characters, Forster takes us perilously near to utter unraveling: "The inarticulate world is closer at hand and readier to resume control as soon as men are tired" (p. 114). Both the wise and the ignorant suffer the fatigues of ordering. The habit of personification, a temporary strategy of human superiority, is regularly exposed by a tireless humor. For the time being, Forster gives himself the privilege of personifying nature in order to see, from a critical perspective, "seven gentlemen . . . dispersed for the interior of other bungalows, to recover their self-esteem and the qualities that distinguished them from each other" (p. 114). The scene spreads:

> All over the city and over much of India the same retreat on the part of humanity was beginning, into cellars, up hills, under trees. April, herald of horrors, is at hand. The sun was returning to his kingdom with power but without beauty—that was the sinister feature. If only there had been beauty! His cruelty would have been tolerable then. Through excess of light, he failed to triumph, he also; in his yellowy-white overflow not only matter, but brightness itself lay drowned. He was not the unattainable friend, either of men or birds or other suns, he

---

4. Albert Camus, *Notebooks, 1942–1951*, trans. Justin O'Brien (New York: Knopf, 1965), pp. 151–52.

was not the eternal promise, the never-withdrawn suggestion that haunts our consciousness; he was merely a creature, like the rest, and so debarred from glory (p. 115).

As he steps down from the sky, Forster shows us how he manages to control the risky pitch that sounds throughout the novel, a bold blending of derision and compassion. At first we are led to think that Forster's description will follow the deterministic line to its reductive finale. By using allegory familiarly, he implies that he has shared the habit of mankind in general to reach the unfamiliar by myths, to control it by such fictions as writing novels. We do not mind being chastened by what we construct. As Aldous Huxley puts it:

> Men long to know the "meaning" of events, to be told the "answer to the riddle of the universe." Christianity provides such an answer and satisfies these "natural" longings: the fact has been regarded by its apologists as a proof of its divine origin and absolute truth. That Christianity should satisfy these longings will not surprise us when we realize that it was Christianity which first implanted them in the human mind and fixed them there as habits.[5]

This is a more comforting feedback than Boum Boum. But Forster qualifies this comfort quickly, though he never dismisses it. As the human world runs from the assault of nature in a contemporary Virgilian simile, Forster exposes the apparent victor as a product of our investment. He is, of course, poking fun at our desire to ennoble our enemy by moralizing it, by dressing it in a beauty which raises the human retreat to a tragic fate. It is a desire that evokes dreams of unity out of tenuous con-

5. Aldous Huxley, *Do What You Will* (London: Chatto and Windus, 1949), p. 292. This is a favorite theme of Büchner, Nietzsche, and Santayana, who writes: "Not that the particular regimen sanctified by Platonic and Christian moralists is at all unacceptable; but they did not require any supernatural assistance to draw it up. They simply received back from revelation the humanism which they had put into it (*The Genteel Tradition at Bay* [New York: Scribner's, 1931], pp. 46–47).

tacts. In an effective scene, Forster describes the "reconciliation" of Ronny and Adela. Their hands are mechanically jolted to a touch:

> Each was too proud to increase the pressure, but neither withdrew it, and a spurious unity descended on them, as local and temporary as the gleam that inhabits a firefly. It would vanish in a moment, perhaps to reappear, but the darkness is alone durable. And the night that encircled them, absolute as it seemed, was itself only a spurious unity, being modified by the gleams of day that leaked up round the edges of the earth, and by the stars (p. 88).

Forster's pathetic fallacies do not console.

But to the lovers the universe seems to have sanctified their alliance; indeed, it seems to have asked for it. By such myths is dignity achieved. In the passage previously cited in which the sun is personified, Forster turns his criticism with only a few touches—the switch to the present tense in the second sentence, the added *he also*, and the *merely* of the last sentence. The use of the present tense to announce the season gives the dimension of timeless and recurring myth. The glorifying personification of the enemy's force, the ordering and naming of the sun with the extravagant terms of human poetry, are balm for the terror of the absurd and the arbitrary, a hymn to the transforming powers of our aesthetic processes. This is the kind of humanism that Robbe-Grillet lambasts in his plea for a new realism. The retreat of humanity is only a faked moral drama, he claims, a "lover's quarrel" between men and nature. From this "false and consoling point of view," claims Robbe-Grillet, "the things around us are like the fairies in the tales, each of whom brought as a gift to the newborn child one of the traits of his future character." Even existential anguish in the face of the absurd is seen by Robbe-Grillet as a mode of salvation: "Since the correspondence between man and things has finally been denounced, the humanist saves his empire by immediately instituting a new form of solidarity, the divorce itself becoming a major path to redemption."

72

Thus tragedy is "the sublimation of a difference." [6] Robbe-Grillet's complaint helps us to distinguish the assumptions about the novel's humanism from its actual nature.

Forster does not allow us to tame the absurd by making its silent incoherence a symptom of tragedy. On the contrary, if there is any salvation at all, it is by comic tolerance of all the divorces we live with and which fill *A Passage to India*. The perspective of a comedy of survival keeps the conversation going between author and character, character and character, author and reader, history and nature, culture and culture, though silence has the only dignity. The heralded terror is playfully undressed by Forster, and our own controls and comforts fall to our ankles. Like us, the sun, "he also," seems unable to resist the temptation to go beyond living to knowing, beyond the humble concrete to a garish abstraction. Like us, he fails to triumph. Like us, he is "merely a creature" who cannot live up to the lovely and mystic names we give him. He descends too close to the human, and he falls, like us, "debarred from glory." But we hear no hallelujahs, no choric moans. In silence he comes up again the next day, since he does not know of a fall that was engineered by the mind of man—more particularly, of a novelist.

We survive without cynicism because Forster has deprived us all, for a moment, of the moralizing relief of pathetic fallacy as well as that of history. Santayana describes well the nature of this humanism:

> I think it is only when he can see the natural origin and limits of the moral sphere that a moralist can be morally sane and just. Blindness to the biological truth about morality is not favourable to purity of moral feeling: it removes all sense of proportion and relativity; it kills charity, humility, and humour; and it shuts the door against that ultimate light which comes to the spirit from the spheres above morality.[7]

6. Alain Robbe-Grillet, *For a New Novel*, trans. Richard Howard (New York: Grove, 1965), pp. 55, 59, 60.
7. Santayana, *The Genteel Tradition*, p. 51.

By refusing to use the nonhuman for salvation or fate, Forster enables us to endure the times. To stay complacently and at length with any man-made perspective might be consoling, but not wise. Man's orders have a way of adjusting all history to the necessary illusion. Even if most periods get bad marks, the process of propitiation goes on:

> What then survives? Oh, a greater purpose, the slow evolution, less slow than it seems, because a thousand years are as yesterday, and consequently Christianity was only, so to speak, established on Wednesday last.[8]

Man tends to patronize the dead—"dear dead women with such hair too"—because it is so much harder to widen his sense of self at the price of saying at the death of others, "I feel chilly and grown old." [9] But to preserve what is human in the past, rather than to imagine it to be greater or less than the living moment, is a compulsion of the humanist.

A dramatic and moving criticism of the comforting state of supermorality rises from Mrs. Moore's dying descent to the sea. She is taunted, as she is affirmed, by the nonhuman world that might, for another author, have remained a final balm for the pettiness of the relationships she has endured:

> The train in its descent through the Vindyas had described a semicircle round Asirgarh. What could she connect it with except its own name? Nothing; she knew no one who lived there. But it had looked at her twice and seemed to say: "I do not vanish." She woke in the middle of the night with a start, for the train was falling over the western cliff. Moonlit pinnacles rushed up at her like the fringes of a sea; then a brief episode of plain, the real sea, and the soupy dawn of Bombay. "I have not seen the right places," she thought, as she saw embayed in the platforms of the Victoria Terminus the end of the rails that had carried her over a continent and could never carry her back. . . . As she drove through the huge city which

8. Forster, "The Consolations of History," in *Abinger Harvest* (London: Edward Arnold, 1953), pp. 193–94.
9. *Ibid.*

the West has built and abandoned with a gesture of despair, she longed to stop, though it was only Bombay, and disentangle the hundred Indias that passed each other in its streets. The feet of the horses moved her on, and presently the boat sailed and thousands of coconut palms appeared all round the anchorage and climbed the hills to wave her farewell. "So you thought an echo was India; you took the Marabar caves as final?" they laughed. "What have we in common with them, or they with Asirgarh? Good-bye!" Then the steamer rounded Colaba, the continent swung about, the cliff of the Ghats melted into the haze of a tropic sea (pp. 209–10).

This is no threshold to transcendence or metamorphosis. The universe mocks our naming and fictionalizes our fictions till the moment we die, and even then we are impelled to say, "I have not seen the right places." When we die we become a name for an order that oversimplifies personality as all costumes of dignity do, a Hindu chant at best: "Esmiss Esmoor, Esmiss Esmoor." That India itself cannot be named except in echoes reveals the irrelevance of history to knowledge. That we must keep on naming defines the human condition. The humanist considers both perspectives. Mrs. Moore's gradual dissolution mocks the politics, moralities, and religions of the West; it even mocks the Western world's dependence on relationships. We realize that a widening wisdom often means a decline in energy; this consciousness will hardly do as a program for the living, who still have to go on in the absence of grace. Her disinterestedness can be, like Godbole's, cruel in a political world. What their ceremonies achieve is a vantage point for criticism, not a groundwork for spiritual affirmation. Godbole's performance chastises Christian seriousness by including merriment, as it reveals the limitations of Fielding's dependence upon daily and human experience, upon the merely secular relationship. While vulnerable to the "joys of form," Fielding recognizes that

> experience can do much, and all that he had learnt in England and Europe was an assistance to him, and helped him towards clarity, but clarity prevented him from experiencing something else (p. 118).

This admission, in turn, moves us to a shared humanity denied us in Godbole's dance. Fielding is neither complacent nor consoled. Forster's rhythm is that of a retreat from the rigidly willed ideologies of the West and from compromising responsibilities and relationships. He fills his pages with metaphors of barriers and backslidings. Their presence leads Fielding to question the worth of a merely serviceable life. All dignity is pulled back to a defensive position. Fielding's "creditable achievement," which he has accomplished without becoming "pedantic or worldly" (p. 191), suddenly does not seem enough. But when Adela speculates that in life, unlike novels, not one is left talking at the end, Fielding is impelled to remind her that we must resist the temptation to abandon conversation in the sun just because it becomes echoes in the anonymous caves of truth. Without our poor chastised fictions we would not be human. And Forster honors Fielding's retort by helping it to survive the inevitable rhythm of humiliation. The scene's atmosphere is too thin to keep Forster for long:

> A friendliness, as of dwarfs shaking hands, was in the air. Both man and woman were at the height of their powers—sensible, honest, even subtle. They spoke the same language, and held the same opinions, and the variety of age and sex did not divide them. Yet they were dissatisfied. When they agreed, "I want to go on living a bit," or, "I don't believe in God," the words were followed by a curious backwash as though the universe had displaced itself to fill up a tiny void, or as though they had seen their own gestures from an immense height—dwarfs talking, shaking hands and assuring each other that they stood on the same footing of insight (p. 264).

Forster does little to elevate the modest gesture of humanism, the attempt to be sensible, honest, subtle. But there is a tiny charity that helps it to persist. When Forster, however provisionally, rises above his characters' habitual perspective to criticize it, he compensates them by relinquishing his own superiority. He had earlier allowed Fielding the privilege of the dramatist viewing his comedy:

Aziz was provocative. Everything he said had an impertinent flavour or jarred. His wings were failing, but he refused to fall without a struggle. He did not mean to be impertinent to Mr. Heaslop, who had never done him harm, but here was an Anglo-Indian who must become a man before comfort could be regained. He did not mean to be greasily confidential to Miss Quested, only to enlist her support; nor to be loud and jolly towards Professor Godbole. A strange quartette—he fluttering to the ground, she puzzled by the sudden ugliness, Ronny fuming, the Brahman observing all three, but with downcast eyes and hands folded, as if nothing was noticeable. A scene from a play, thought Fielding, who now saw them from the distance across the garden grouped among the blue pillars of his beautiful hall (p. 77).

Forster checks Fielding's temporary advantage, as he checks his own, by first giving Aziz a sense of separation from his own phrases that makes him an audience critical of his drama. Such precedence leads us to ask how far dignity can be enhanced by *not* being absorbed into the comedy. Is the evident poise of Mrs. Moore and Professor Godbole a permanent superiority? When Fielding is involved up to his neck, do we think less of his wisdom? For Forster, as for his most sensitive characters, there is no stopping point at nobility. The will is humbled by the spirit, the moral by the mystic, but these terms are explored by the stuttering word and felt by the faltering handshake.

Suppose India has the advantage over the West of a patient realism:

In Europe life retreats out of the cold, and exquisite fireside myths have resulted—Balder, Persephone—but here the retreat is from the source of life, the treacherous sun, and no poetry adorns it because disillusionment cannot be beautiful (pp. 210–11).

"India," says Forster, "fails to accommodate" men who "desire that joy shall be graceful and sorrow august and infinity have a form" (p. 211). The forms Europe lives by are romances of morality. What Adela resented in Aziz's lie about the toddy palm

being a serpent was a mysticism that neither elevated nor consoled, the creation of a romance without the order of a morality.
April's anarchy, which Forster heralded a hundred pages earlier,
explodes the pretense of naming. And "to prove to society how
little its categories impress her" (p. 217), India's nature creates a
beautiful and neutral creature which we call "untouchable." The
universe seems to taunt our poetry as it escapes our ordering
grasp. It dissolves our personifications as it refuses to be made
into our image. What then can we make of India's own poetry?
Forster's nature abhors a dialectical vacuum. Godbole's poetry
and Aziz's, so different from each other, effectively criticize by
their easy flow the way in which Western literature has been
divorced from its sources. The purity of impression, "a night-
ingale between two worlds of dust" (p. 106), would seem to
spring the Western coil. But if their poetry did in fact annihilate
instead of criticize, it would be invulnerable to humor and, hence,
an unconvincing agent of humanism. The funny vanities and
outbursts that fill Aziz's sickroom are in their own way as irrelevant to nature as the Western personification. They seem to
imitate April's anarchy, but they are the base of the mystic
sentimentalism that follows. The poem, says Forster,

> had no connection with anything that had gone before, but it
> came from his heart and spoke to theirs. They were over-
> whelmed by its pathos; pathos, they agreed, is the highest quality
> in art; a poem should touch the hearer with a sense of his own
> weakness, and should institute some comparison between man-
> kind and flowers. The squalid bedroom grew quiet; the silly
> intrigues, the gossip, the shallow discontent were stilled, while
> words accepted as immortal filled the indifferent air. Not as a
> call to battle, but as a calm assurance came the feeling that India
> was one; Moslem; always had been; an assurance that lasted
> until they looked out of the door (p. 105).

Any poetry practices its own brand of illusion. The myth of
Balder has become the myth of Moslem unity. The naïveté of the
idea that "a poem . . . should institute some comparison between mankind and flowers" touches us as we imagine it in a

handbook on reading Homer. And the tone of this line is both its weakness and its strength. That is the point. Forster, no more than this poetry, calls us to battle. For a while, we feel free from the moral stress of much Western art. But, lest we forget that words are not immortal, Forster reminds us that they can only be accepted as such. We are brought back to the realities and responsibilities of a political and divided world by the view of disunity outside the door. This effective comic descent is the same that continually fells Forster's own vision. It is imitated in a later post-trial scene in which we seem to see a small Hindu-Moslem entente. Like the dwarfed Adela and Fielding, Das and Aziz shake hands across barriers of irony. Forster comments:

> Between people of distant climes there is always the possibility of romance, but the various branches of Indians know too much about each other to surmount the unknowable easily. The approach is prosaic. "Excellent," said Aziz, patting a stout shoulder and thinking, "I wish they did not remind me of cow-dung"; Das thought, "Some Moslems are very violent."
> They smiled wistfully, each spying the thought in the other's heart, and Das, the more articulate, said: "Excuse my mistakes, realize my limitations. Life is not easy as we know it on the earth" (p. 267).

In the best humanist pattern, personality resists full expression and confession full truth as tongues fork into conversation.[10]

Aziz's attraction to poetry, we remember, is that it dissolves distinctions by raising individual tragedy to universal pathos. This is the function of its romance—to overrate, for better and for worse, the possibilities of communion between man and man, man and his universe, culture and culture, history and apocalypse, the body and the spirit. After separating himself from Hindu interests (we see a comedy of competition between two poets,

---

10. In his book on Forster, Frederick Crews notes: "The refusal to abandon personality, which is the strongest bond between Aziz and the Westerners in the novel, turns out to be a severe limitation in their apparatus for grasping transcendent truth" (*The Perils of Humanism* [Princeton: Princeton Univ. Press, 1962], p. 153).

Godbole and Aziz), Aziz attempts a poem on "the decay of Islam and the brevity of love" (p. 268). Then he tries a satire. But his heart is not in it. The difference between this shortened series of attempts and those that Flaubert relates is marked by the distance between the sympathy of humor and the precision of analysis. Aziz longs for the romance of populism; overcoming convention and manner, it would be "the song of the future" that could "transcend creed" (p. 268). But Forster inevitably stops short of historical recommendation. There is no Zionism on the horizon. The dreams of unity that inhabit the minds of his characters tumble, and the hands that touch fall apart. But even as they tumble, dreams criticize our actuality. Forster describes this relation succinctly: "The poem for Mr. Bhattacharya never got written, but it had an effect" (p. 268). Hamidullah's practical and philosophical sense of proportion checks Aziz's dreams of unity, but Hamidullah is himself moved by Aziz's passion. In a counterdirection, the suggestion of Aziz's subject for poetry, "The Indian lady as she is and not as she is supposed to be," is belittled by the question "I am determined to write poetry. The problem is, about what?" And all this is succeeded by a rash and mean divorce from Fielding.

No experience, no word, can shake the echo of nonmeaning. No relationship can shake the shadow of divorce. Romance unchecked by evidence caused Aziz's difficulties; now his dream of love fosters suspicion of the foreigner and his friend. It is the oldest of tensions, that between brother and brotherhood, between the difficulties of loving one's neighbor and dreams of love. But Forster goes beyond a simple dialectic. Even in dreams, Aziz's love distinguishes between national and universal. What Forster is ultimately telling us is that poetry or religion, where love may dwell without tension, cannot further the kind of personal relationship that is the center of the humanist novel, the relationship that barely holds on with dwarfed hands. Explicitly and in allegories of nature mocking man, Forster indicates that Western poetry, religion, and myth help us to order the universe and to relieve us from absurdity by yoking together man and man, man and nature, with imperative fictitious commands. Mrs. Moore's "Oh, why is everything still my duty? . . . Was he in the cave and were you in the cave and on and on . . . and Unto us a Son is born, unto us a Child is given . . . and am I good and is he bad and are we saved?" (p. 205) clearly reveals how her society's morality depends on this romance. It excuses relationships like that of Adela and Ronny.

In contrast, Indian poetry deals with the absurd by dissolving distinctions between man and flower. It relieves anxieties brought on by the compulsion to moral order with the perspective of pathos, that view which sees all victory as fate. Aziz's divorce of poetry from friendship, with the separation of grace from justice, is an agonizing human pattern. He abstracts Fielding into a public representation, into one who has "thrown nets over his dreams" (p. 268), in the same way that Aziz is abstracted by the Westerners. And this historicizing of personality is in the cause of a willed dream of one India. "No device," says Forster, "has been found by which . . . private decencies can be transmitted to public affairs." [11] The personal and spontaneous affection between Mrs. Moore and Aziz is useless in a court of law. The humanist's recognition of the absurd is essentially the recognition of this separation. Forster habitually reminds us:

> Love is a great force in private life; it is indeed the greatest of all things: but love in public affairs does not work. It has been tried again and again: by the Christian civilisations of the Middle Ages, and also by the French Revolution, a secular movement which reasserted the Brotherhood of Man. And it has always failed. The idea that nations should love one another, or that business concerns or marketing boards should love one another, or that a man in Portugal should love a man in Peru of whom he has never heard—it is absurd, unreal, dangerous. It leads us into perilous and vague sentimentalism. "Love is what is needed," we chant, and then sit back and the world goes on as before. The fact is that we can only love what we know personally. And we cannot know much. In public affairs, in the

11. Forster, "What I Believe," in *Two Cheers for Democracy*, p. 74.

rebuilding of civilisation, something much less dramatic and emotional is needed, namely, tolerance. Tolerance is a very dull virtue. It is boring. Unlike love, it has always had a bad press. It is negative. . . . No one has ever written an ode to tolerance.[12]

Neither Fielding's morally bound decency nor Godbole's merry spiritualism and modest self-extension, which threaten to exclude nothing, can bridge the gap between public and private. In each case, "come, come, come" is a process, not an end, that suffers in translation. "Still," as Godbole touchingly puts it, "it is more than I am myself" (p. 291). Neither love nor art can shape history, order society, or raise relationships to social or spiritual completion. For the humanist, therefore, love and art are free from determined service to cause and abstraction. This is only a consolation for unfulfilled dreams of what they might do as apocalypse. Yet the humanist novelist cannot yield to Mrs. Moore's dream of Flaubertian retreat:

> What is the use of personal relationships when everyone brings less and less to them? I feel we ought all to go back into the desert for centuries and try and get good. I want to begin at the beginning (p. 197).

The humanist cannot grant us the dignity and simplicity we long for in the presence of human need and identity. He sees, with George Eliot, that all beginnings are fictive. In an antic Godbolean dance, Forster might fling up his hands and say with Mrs. Moore, "As if anything can be said!" (p. 200). But then, to

12. Forster, "Tolerance," in *ibid.*, p. 45. It is interesting to compare Freud's statement: "The commandment, 'Love thy neighbour as thyself,' is the strongest defence against human aggressiveness and an excellent example of the unpsychological proceedings of the cultural super-ego. The commandment is impossible to fulfil; such an enormous inflation of love can only lower its value, not get rid of the difficulty. Civilization pays no attention to all this; it merely admonishes us that the harder it is to obey the precept the more meritorious it is to do so" (*Civilization and Its Discontents*, trans. James Strachey [New York: Norton, 1961], p. 90).

remind us what it is to be human, refusing both glory and despair, he says it.[13]

13. Crews comments on the consistent and negative pattern of Forster's temperament in *A Passage to India:* "Here at last, Forster accepts with his whole imagination the destructive ironies of his humanism" (*Perils of Humanism,* p. 179).

The crowd is untruth.

Sören Kierkegaard

The invention of the devil. If we are possessed by the devil, it cannot be by one, for then we should live, at least here on earth, quietly, as with God, in unity, without contradiction, without reflection, always sure of the man behind us. His face would not frighten us, for as diabolical beings we would, if somewhat sensitive to the sight, be clever enough to prefer to sacrifice a hand in order to keep his face covered with it. . . . Only a crowd of devils could account for our earthly misfortunes. . . . We still do not arrive at any state of well-being so long as the many devils are within us.

Franz Kafka

"When we hear the hairsplitting metaphysicians and prophets of the afterworld speak, we others feel indeed that we are the 'poor in spirit,' but that ours is the heavenly kingdom of change, with spring and autumn, summer and winter, and theirs the afterworld, with its gray, everlasting frosts and shadows." Thus soliloquized a man as he walked in the morning sunshine, a man who in his pursuit of history has constantly changed not only his mind but his heart. In contrast to the metaphysicians, he is happy to harbor in himself not an "immortal soul" but many *mortal* souls.

Friedrich Nietzsche

CHAPTER FIVE

The Brothers Karamazov:
Reality as Miracle

Forster keeps all orders vulnerable by describing conversation that comes unwound and drifts into deafness. It is a common assumption of the humanist novelist that conversation, by which we must live, is even at its most serious an absurd tableau, a parody of what we feel. Behind this poignant comedy is the persistent realization that we can never fully know each other, but that, in Kierkegaard's phrase, our "object of faith is the reality of another."[1] In Dostoevsky's novels the difficulties of communication are parodied by the pantomime that effects what the word cannot. Like the gospel inversions of power, the small gesture surprises and humiliates the prosecuting word and the idealist's legends. The giving of a tiny onion shames all the static brilliance of Ivan's dialectic as much as it satirizes Mrs. Khokhlakov's "charitable" gold mines; the miracle of marriage in the Cana of Galilee vision criticizes Ivan's celibate protestations against the world's misery; Father Zossima's life overcomes Ivan's prosecutions, and his image overcomes that of Ivan's fluent devil;

---

1. Kierkegaard, "Postscript to Philosophical Fragments," in *A Kierkegaard Anthology*, ed. Robert Bretall (Princeton: Princeton Univ. Press, 1947), p. 230.

Christ's kiss competes with the syllogisms of the Grand Inquisitor as Father Zossima's prostration at the feet of Dmitri darkens the articulate counsels of Ivan and Miusov; the law court's logic is flattened by Alyosha's final invitation to the children. Everywhere the "humanitarian" rhetoric of socialism and atheism and that of the papist church intent on divorcing man from Christ is made uncomfortable by silence. The mute Jesus distresses his inquisitor: "He saw that the Prisoner had been listening intently to him all the time, looking gently into his face and evidently not wishing to say anything in reply." [2] And Ivan's unwitting recognition in his legend of the superiority of the act to the word and the dream gives rise to Alyosha's famous retort: "Your poem is in praise of Jesus and not in his disparagement—as you wanted it to be" (I, 305). But while the quiet modesty of pantomime is descriptive of our hope, the gesticulations of the "clowns of shame" (I, 46) are symptomatic of our fate.

Discontinuity of conversation is the rhythm of our hell. The unobtrusive narrator of *The Devils* describes the scene from which Stavrogin has melodramatically departed with Mary Lebyatkin:

> They said little, though: they mostly uttered astonished cries. I am afraid I can't very well remember the exact order in which it all happened at the time, for everything was in confusion. Mr. Verkhovensky was shouting something in French and throwing up his hands in amazement, but Mrs. Stavrogin was too preoccupied with her own thoughts to take any notice of him. Even Mr. Drozdov muttered something abruptly and rapidly. But Peter Verkhovensky was more excited than anyone; he was trying desperately to convince Mrs. Stavrogin about something, gesticulating wildly, but for a long time I could not make out what he was talking about. He also addressed Mrs. Drozdov and Lisa, and even shouted something in passing to his father in his excitement—in a word, he kept rushing about the room. Mrs. Stavrogin, all flushed, jumped up from her chair

---

2. Dostoevsky, *The Brothers Karamazov*, trans. David Magarshack, 2 vols. (Baltimore: Penguin, 1958), II, 308. Future references will be to this edition and will be noted in the text.

and shouted to Mrs. Drozdov, "Did you hear? Did you hear what he said to her just now?" But Mrs. Drozdov was not in a condition to reply. She just muttered something with a wave of the hand. The poor woman had her own worries.[3]

In this daily hell, "all men are separated into self-contained units, everyone crawls into his own hole, everyone separates himself from his neighbor, hides himself away and hides away everything he possesses, and ends up by keeping himself at a distance from people and keeping other people at a distance from him" (I, 357). And in these monasteries of the heart, justification replaces conversation. Christ gives offense by paradox in the service of a necessary higher communication, that of active love. But for those who perpetuate their own infernos, giving offense may be a pleasure (I, 46–47), a consolation, a self-righteous judgment. Obsessive self-justification is the masochism that links the underground man, Fyodor Karamazov, and the unconverted Dmitri. Their lacerating confessions do not contradict the state of spiritual translation; they continually precede it. Alyosha, seeking "a higher justice" (II, 398) for Father Zossima's corpse, which has been moved by Ivan's indictment (I, 284; II, 400), adopts the language of prosecution and vindication before accepting the premise that no measurable equations can refute the impressive truths of law, logic, and speculation.

Dostoevsky's metaphysics remains centrally humanist in the novel, not because it gives spiritual solutions to ethical problems, but because it casts suspicion on demands for solutions. When Ivan maintains, "We have first of all to solve the eternal questions" (I, 272), he relieves himself of confronting the dilemmas of his own life. Ivan insists on miracles from reason. The self-indulgent words of prosecution that flow from his room and from the law courts of the world help us to escape the terror of private conversations. These ex cathedra pronouncements try to control the domestic spaces between dream and actuality. Their

3. Dostoevsky, *The Devils*, trans. David Magarshack (Baltimore: Penguin, 1953), p. 192.

pretense of primal order and knowledge, compensating us for the state of ethical and spiritual divorce, perpetuates it. If Ivan can love neither man nor God, at least he can judge. As judge, he avoids that consuming guilt by association, which, as Orwell in a slightly different context reminds us, is "the inevitable price of fastening one's love upon other individuals." [4] To Ivan, Dmitri is guilty because he is human. The recognition of the particular would call for a difficult dealing with life instead of a speculation on its meaning. Ivan's impasse comforts him as much as it distresses him. "Christ's love for men is, in a way, a miracle that is impossible on earth" (I, 277), and imperfect love compromises the purity of Christ's example. But Christ refuses the temptations to provide solutions, while the Grand Inquisitor uses temptations to justify solution by "miracle, mystery, and authority." He, not Christ, drives the act of love to dreams.

Those who dream of heroic solutions are, ironically, those who demand to see the miracle of romantic love. Father Zossima explains:

> Romantic love yearns for an immediate act of heroism that can be achieved rapidly and that everyone can see. This sort of love really reaches a point where a man will even sacrifice his life provided his ordeal doesn't last long and is over quickly just as though it took place on a stage, and provided all are looking on and applauding (I, 64).

Love that forgoes dreams for daily deeds, apocalypse for this life, is embarrassed by theatricality. Charity and grace that can be given on the scale of a tiny onion are the hidden miracles that define the real. The dreamers want only recompense for their human investment; God owes them a world. The egoism of the apocalyptist of love is evident in this demand for a sign:

> I must have retribution or I shall destroy myself. And retribution not somewhere in the infinity of space and time, but here

4. George Orwell, "Reflections on Gandhi," in *A Collection of Essays of George Orwell* (New York: Doubleday, 1954), pp. 182–83.

on earth, and so that I could see it myself. . . . If it all happens without me, it will be too unfair. . . . I want to see with my own eyes the lion lie down with the lamb and the murdered man rise up and embrace his murderer (I, 285–86).

Ivan demands a miracle impossible on earth—that God take back freedom and obliterate injustice to save us from the necessity of love. Ivan's depth and pathos and the constant betrayal of his spiritualism in his legends where hosanna counts more than science elevate him far beyond Mrs. Khokhlakov, Smerdyakov, and Rakitin. But by their weaknesses we are meant to know him. Nothing so clearly reflects the egoism of Ivan's expectations as Mrs. Khokhlakov's chastisement of Father Zossima's stinking corpse—"What conduct" (II, 401)—or the horror of their consequences as Smerdyakov's murder of his father.[5] The ethical patronization of the spiritual is a distortion of Ivan's claim, but it is also a reminder of it. The arithmetic of Mrs. Khokhlakov, whose concept of love adds up to an offer to Dmitri of work in a gold mine, is related to that of Ivan; two plus two must equal four. This is the mathematics of retribution.

Ivan resists the recognition that heaven can only be travestied on earth. His devil parodies Dostoevsky's definition of the real equation (two plus two often equals five) by yearning for an earthly realism that consoles because it is registered in "clear outlines. . . . Everything is a formula, here everything is geometry" (II, 750–51). The metaphysical realm (and, by extension, the psychological), the devil complains, is measured by an "indeterminate equation" (II, 751). Ivan admits the limitations of the Euclidean mind; he asks how he can "be expected to solve problems which are not of this world" (I, 274). But who is asking him to solve them? He hangs on to this expectation in order to escape the more difficult responsibility of loving his brothers in this world. He insists on measuring the spiritual with

5. Albert Camus links Ivan and Smerdyakov by underlining the agonizing paradox that to become God means to accept crime (*The Rebel: An Essay on Man in Revolt*, trans. Anthony Bower [New York: Knopf, 1958], p. 119).

the ethical. But harmony on earth, which is only an apocalyptic sum, is not the answer to the earthly equation. Ironically, the devil's comic desire to exchange his metaphysical shabbiness for the body of one plump merchant's wife effectively criticizes Ivan's desire to suspend this world of particulars in eternal solutions. If Ivan's new utopian man has declared his independence from gods, why does he "want the sanction of truth" (II, 764)? The devil astutely reveals the uses to which Ivan, like the Grand Inquisitor, puts the spiritual. Ivan needs it to escape from his neighbor, his brother, his father, his lover. The seeds of rebellion breed a state of abstraction, and that is why Ivan's recognitions are so poignant: "One can't go on living in a state of rebellion, and I want to live" (I, 287). His satanic humanitarian tells Ivan what he knows but will not admit:

> I keep you dangling between belief and disbelief by turns, and I don't mind admitting that I have a reason for it. It's the new method, sir. For when you lose your faith in me completely, you will at once begin assuring me to my face that I'm not a dream, but do really exist. . . . And then I shall have attained my object, and my object is an honorable one. I shall sow a tiny grain of faith in you and it will grow into an oak tree—and such an oak tree that, sitting on it, you will long to join "the hermits in the wilderness and the chaste virgins," for at heart you long for it greatly (II, 759).

From believing in the reality of an abstract, unambiguous enemy, it is only a short distance to the desired release into history, away from the present where there are only attitudes and not solutions. Love in the wilderness is pure. Ivan would fall for the temptation that his Christ resists, and he would be spared the task of inventing doubles who, as sparring partners, cast as much doubt on his own reality as they create belief in it.

Ivan injects religious irony into his obsessive refrain when he says, "To love a man, it's necessary that he should be hidden, for as soon as he shows his face, love is gone" (I, 276). A real devil would sanction him to hide his face from men. Typically, it is the hidden God that bedevils Ivan. Ivan demands to see his face because he needs someone tangible on whom to blame the world's parents; God owes a better sum to Ivan and his children. Yet Ivan's suffering children are faceless. If by syllogisms of injustice God can be separated from his world, brother from brother, parent from child, and man from Christ, then Ivan can stay in his room forever, a prisoner of just protestations. If he divides, he conquers, controls, and judges. "As a dreamer of dreams," says Pascal, "Joseph foretells only." Ivan is a Joseph in willing bondage. Father Zossima reminds us of the Joseph who recognizes his brothers and father and makes them see his face, who changes dreams of retribution into active love (I, 344). He plants a single corn of wheat and, like Alyosha, does not wait for manna.

The recognition at Illusha's funeral is of a particular face, hand, personality. It is imagination coupled with memory rather than with philosophy that allows us to live in the face of absurdity. The novel teaches what the tract cannot, and "one good memory . . . may be the instrument of our salvation" (II, 911). Ivan is mnemonically structured by intellectual creations; his biography is remembered as the story of the Grand Inquisitor, the devil's legends. He can exist only in his stories, since literature protects his life. But literature also cuts him off from life. His plague, in Camus's words, is "to live in company with a memory that serves no purpose." The deliberately prosaic memoirs of Father Zossima's life parallel and illuminate the drama of Dmitri's life. Dmitri's dream of the suffering babe is a memory, as the re-creation of Cana of Galilee is for Alyosha; in each, the miraculous marriage of the self to others through suffering and gladness affirms the necessity and reality of Christ, who leads men to active love of others. We need not be obsessively turned upon and tortured by the possessed self. The sympathy that puts a pillow under Dmitri's head could transform Ivan's nightmare into a "good dream" (II, 596–97). By accusing Christ, the Grand Inquisitor can father the world's children. By accusing God and the parents of the world, Ivan can claim the children's innocence for himself. The absurdist's solution to absurdity is to abstract the self and others into syllogisms of cause and effect. While Ivan rejects the world in the name of all its suffering children, Alyosha can accept the world for the sake of each child; he knows that the children are not innocent, that to be born is to relinquish that possibility. We can apply Dmitri's description of Katya to Ivan: "She loves her own virtue, not me" (I, 135).

The vocabularies of apocalypse and prosecution indicate that words are substituting for acts. The words of parable, sermon, and spiritual biography are finally unimpressive because they carry no burden of justification. They are meant only to motivate lives. But Ivan's dialectic, like that of the prosecuting attorney, is a disguised monologue that swells the particular to a great abstraction. Rakitin is interested in making of Dmitri's suffering a case history, and Ivan in making of a suffering child an indictment against God's world; the prosecuting attorney creates out of one man's trial a national guilt and a cultural punishment. Enormous complexities are avoided by such unrestricted anger.

The sacrifice, in word and dream, of the particular to the general for the sake of a final and forceful judgment is the major movement of the absurdist, the fantastic man. The devil recognizes his double as a man who, like him, "suffers from the fantastic" (II, 750) because he cannot sound his words outside the monastery of abstract humanitarianism. Ivan's divorce from life enables him to philosophize about situation and self, to substitute pity and protest for love and act. Kierkegaard describes the sentimentality of the fantastical as a malady of the age as well as of one man:

> Generally, the fantastical is that which so carries a man out into the infinite that it merely carries him away from himself and therewith prevents him from returning to himself.
> So when feeling is simply volatilized more and more, at last becoming a sort of abstract sentimentality which is so inhuman that it does not apply to any person, but inhumanly participates feelingly, so to speak, in the fate of one or another abstraction, e.g. that of mankind *in abstracto* . . . he becomes in a way

infinitized, but not in such a way that he becomes more and more himself, for he loses himself more and more.[6]

As he loses himself, he certainly does not gain his soul. Dostoevsky's major intention in the novel is to dramatize the transvaluation of the terms *real* and *fantastic*, which were both aesthetically and psychologically crucial concerns for him. We are meant to be impressed by Ivan's noble elevation of psychological to political. Here is a man who does not overlook the needs and facts of his time. He is a realist. But this "realist" is lord only of his own needs and his own facts. What we feel to be most real about Ivan is not his politics but the sense that they do not really convince him. His ideal of the new man produces only caricatures like Rakitin, rather than Dmitri of active love. If Dmitri's position of "head over heels" were merely boastful sensuality, he, like his father, would also be a caricature. But that position enables him to kiss the hem of God. The real cannot be felt unless it contains the absurd contradiction between what is and what man feels must be.

Dostoevsky relies on Alyosha as a humanizing agent of conversion between two actors of absurdity, one of the flesh and the other of the intellect.[7] Alyosha's greatest power, that of listening, exposes melodramas of confession. His listening leads both Ivan and Dmitri from confession to conversation, though Ivan, we imagine, will never be able to live by it. When Dmitri is stripped, he sheds his cloak of fantasy. He dies unto himself, but only to live with others, to bear fruit. "A new man has arisen in me" (II, 694), he tells Alyosha; Dostoevsky parodies the new man of the radical socialists by interiorizing the Second Coming. For the Nihilists expect new men, gods of purpose, to set society right. Dmitri's new man is nonpolitical and nonphilosophical. He is not

6. Kierkegaard, *Sickness unto Death*, in *Fear and Trembling and Sickness unto Death*, ed. and trans. Walter Lowrie (New York: Doubleday, 1955), p. 213. The fantastic man bears within him a good dose of what the critic Dobrolyubov calls "Oblomovitis."

7. He doubtlessly feels defensive about Ivan and Dmitri, as George Eliot does about Mordecai's sympathies and Deronda's reality.

a solution but an attitude, and Dmitri knows that attitudes remain vulnerable to backsliding. His logic is more pragmatic than all the syllogisms of Ivan. God and Grushenka exist because without love Dmitri cannot live and men cannot love each other without God. Dmitri's cry "If they banish God from the earth we shall need him under the earth" (II, 694) converts desperation to faith and offsets Ivan's Voltairean game ("If God did not exist . . ." [I, 274]), to say nothing of how uncomfortable this displacement would make the devil feel. Dmitri can live without justice but not without love. The fact that active love can assimilate the absurd while social planning cannot is the miracle that defines the real.

In Dostoevsky's novel, the blasphemous humanitarian calling for universal justice secretly idealizes the potential of man's institutions for curing history with a science of ethics. For this fantastic man, who precedes the realist, the fact humiliates faith; for the realist, the fact proves the necessity of faith. Nothing so effectively reveals the widening levels of communication as the trial, in which the buzz of Dmitri's hymn makes the whole question of justice seem incidental. Dmitri's fate has been impervious to prosecution from the moment he cries out on the way to Mokroye: "Lord, do not judge me, because I've condemned myself. Do not judge me because I love Thee" (II, 485). The law's logic fosters a prosecuting psychology that may guess the act but not the motivation, or arrogantly assume the motivation but miss the act. Its workings seem impressive; its verdicts are wrong. It cannot understand how the world's injustice and absurdity fling Dmitri into moments of gladness as they crucify Ivan.

Frank Kermode points out some dangers of the transvaluating spirit when it is operative outside the novel, when fiction hardens to myth and history and the intention is that "the world [be] changed to conform with fiction." [8] One example of how litera-

8. Frank Kermode, *The Sense of an Ending* (New York: Oxford Univ. Press, 1967), p. 109.

ture can condemn life is the prosecuting attorney's famous complaint about Russia's lack of cultural dignity: Europe has its Hamlets, "but so far we still have our Karamazovs!" (II, 845). The real Dmitri Karamazov has been shamed by his caricatured abstractions as has his wild ride to Mokroye been humiliated by the cunning troika metaphor.[9] The harsh apocalyptic tone of Dostoevsky's notes and diaries, in which the danger of transvaluating is evident, reveals an interesting irony. Outside the novel, Dostoevsky regularly succumbs to an unqualified absurdist vision. The novel enables him to reclaim the real.[10] There is very little difference between the George Eliot of the *Letters* and the novelist. Fiction merely enables her to dramatize her moral sensibilities. But Dostoevsky's epistolary tone is more like that of the underground man, caught between a recognition of the new man's absurdity and an inability to enlist an active love. Dostoevsky teases us with the constant self-identification of an "evil and exaggeratedly passionate nature." Like Dmitri, he admits that "in all things I go to the uttermost extreme; my life long I have never been acquainted with moderation." [11] Without humanist fiction's mediating demands, Dostoevsky must aggressively defend his personal search for ultimate answers:

9. R. L. Jackson speaks of Dmitri's representative quality as a Dostoevsky and a Russia seeking moral structure and form. As a child-man, Dmitri gropes toward the new man, a state that can never be permanent. This vulnerability plays well into the prosecutor's hands ("Dmitrij Karamazov and the 'Legend,'" *Slavic and East European Journal*, IX, no. 3 [1965], 256–67).

10. It is interesting to place this inversion next to the suspended solutions of Balzac and Dickens, to whom Dostoevsky has often been compared. Balzac and Dickens are among those rarest of novelists who are at home in both absurdist and humanist worlds, balancing them in their major novels. Each revels in the independent vitality of his characters—the strongest distinguishing mark of the humanist; each, like many absurdists, conceives of the novel as an autonomous world that punishes civilization's compromises by idealizing innocence. But both, delighting in their saturation in the society they condemn, stop short in their novels of any compulsive transvaluation, like that of Dostoevsky, which must make of injustice a proof of Christ.

11. Dostoevsky to Apollon Nikolayevitch Maikov, Aug. 16, 1867, *Letters of Fyodor Dostoevsky*, trans. E. C. Mayne (New York: McGraw-Hill, 1964), p. 119.

One may set up any paradox one likes, and so long as one doesn't carry it to its ultimate conclusion, everyone will think it most subtle, witty, *comme il faut;* but once blurt out the last word, and quite frankly (not by implication) declare: "This is the Messiah!" why, nobody will believe in you any more—for it was so silly of you to push your idea to its ultimate conclusion! If many a famous wit, such as Voltaire, had resolved for once to rout all hints, allusions, and esotericisms by force of his genuine beliefs, to show the real Himself, he would quite certainly not . . . have been laughed at. For man instinctively avoids saying his last word; he has a prejudice against "thoughts said." [12]

In the novel, Dostoevsky may be critical of making aesthetic sport of ethical positions—the prosecutor's games of psychology; Fyodor Karamazov's games of offense; the political and sociological games of Rakitin and Miusov; the philosophical games of the Enlightenment as they drift down to the devils, Smerdyakov and little Kolya—but he never obliterates these actions with the last metaphysical word. It is the socialistic and atheistic vocabulary of prosecution and case history, the environmental sociologists and planners of happiness, that make claims for the man-god. Alyosha trades vision for memory and the last verbalization for an invitation to eat pancakes in the face of death. Underground, Dmitri's hymn will have to be intoned over and over again. The novel's truth is only a vulnerable testing, a compromised action. The extreme humility of the gospel is a necessary counterweight to the "final" pronouncement of the new men.

The Dostoevsky of the notes and diaries, unlike the novelist, intends not to continue life, but to substitute for it; he allies himself with Ivan, who insists that paradox become resolution, not resignation. Yet, like the underground man, Dostoevsky is continually reminding the environmentalists of the natural enmity between reason and morality,[13] a recognition that, in both the censored *Notes from Underground* and the "unfinished" *Brothers*

12. Dostoevsky to Vsevolod Solovyov, July, 1876, *ibid.*, p. 228.
13. See, for example, Dostoevsky, *The Diary of a Writer*, ed. and trans. Boris Brasol (New York: Scribner's, 1949), I, 13.

Karamazov, prepares for a religious perspective. Directed against the "Europe of Mill, Darwin, and Strauss," [14] however, his blueprint for a resurrected Russia, his Russian "solution," betrays Dmitri's suffering as much as the prosecutor's cultural imperative, "Do not disappoint Russia" (II, 852), betrays understanding. Dostoevsky himself becomes the inquisitor, the prosecutor. The particularity of character, the individuality of the Christian vision and conversion, and the singularity of the falling corn of wheat are all forgotten as the Russian personality yields to the "Russian *idea*" and the speech to the children to a "universal mission." [15] Whereas in the novel the transvaluation of *fantastic* and *real* is an agent of peace, in Dostoevsky's Eastern question it becomes a mode of political defense and attack, an agent of war:

> Oh, of course, you might laugh at all these "fancies" about the Russian mission; however, tell me: do not all Russians desire the resurrection of the Slavs precisely on this basis—precisely for the sake of their full individual liberty and the resurrection of their spirit—and not at all for the purpose that Russia may politically acquire them and, through them, increase her political power? [16]

Dostoevsky's spiritual totalitarianism allows him to say, "Without war people grow torpid in riches and comfort, and lose the power of thinking and feeling nobly." This kind of recommendation could never derive from the tone of George Eliot's "Jewish solution," whatever her degree of cultural abstraction. She is interested in chastening the near by means of a larger, alien view; Dostoevsky is interested in imposing an enlarged view of the near onto an alien world which he impoverishes and reduces. As we might suspect, his vision, like those of Mrs. Khokhlakov, the prosecuting attorney, and the Grand Inquisitor, is of the salvation of "whole races," not of "individuals." [17] This historical inflation is, in the words of

14. *Ibid.,* p. 150.
15. *Ibid.,* p. 361.
16. *Ibid.,* p. 362.
17. Dostoevsky to Sofia Alexandrovna, Aug. 17, 1870, *Letters,* p. 206.

Lévi-Strauss, the "last refuge of a transcendental humanism: as if men could regain the illusion of liberty on the plane of the 'we' merely by giving up the 'I's' that are too obviously wanting in consistency." [18]

Outside the novel, Dostoevsky, like Ivan, cannot leave heaven where it is:

> It may be said that this is a fantasy, that this "Russian answer to the problem" is "the Kingdom of Heaven," and is only possible in the Kingdom of Heaven. Yes, the Stivas would grow very angry were the Kingdom of Heaven to come. However, the fact itself should be taken into account that this fantasy of "the Russian solution to the problem" is incomparably less fantastic and infinitely more plausible than the European solution. Such men, i.e., "Vlases," we have already seen, we rather often perceive them now among all classes; but, thus far, we have seen nowhere their "future man," and he himself promised to come only after crossing rivers of blood. [19]

Necessity is continually the totalitarian plea:

> Ours is a sacred idea, and our war is not "the eternal bestial instinct of imprudent nations," but specifically the first step toward the realization of that perpetual peace in which we are happy to believe—toward the attainment *in reality* of international fellowship and of *truly* humane welfare! [20]

Reality has become whatever propaganda needs it to be.

The novelist's obsessive epistemological transvaluating is most obviously debased in the service of political or sociological polemic, but a subtler debasement occurs in his frankly aesthetic apologies. Very quickly he forgets that the novel's truth lies in the consciousness of its fiction. One of his most famous definitions of the novel's realism is his defense of *The Idiot:*

18. Claude Lévi-Strauss, *The Savage Mind*, trans. George Weidenfeld (Chicago: Univ. of Chicago Press, 1966), p. 262.
19. Dostoevsky, *Diary*, II, 624.
20. *Ibid.*, p. 668.

I have my own idea about art, and it is this: What most people regard as fantastic and lacking in universality, *I* hold to be the inmost essence of truth. Arid observation of everyday trivialities I have long ceased to regard as realism—it is quite the reverse. In any newspaper one takes up, one comes across reports of wholly authentic facts, which nevertheless strike one as extraordinary. Our writers regard them as fantastic, and take no account of them; and yet they are the truth, for they are facts. But who troubles to observe, record, describe them? They happen every day and every moment, therefore they are not "exceptional. . . . " But is not my fantastic "Idiot" the very dailiest truth? Precisely such characters *must* exist in those strata of our society which have divorced themselves from the soil—which actually are becoming fantastic.[21]

This perspective could be used to describe *The Brothers Karamazov*. A whole society divorced from its fathers is fantastic.[22] This observation satisfies Dostoevsky because it seems sociologically real. When society's discontinuous motions are recorded in fiction, critics complain that they seem merely grotesque. Dostoevsky plays their game when he justifies his imaginations by facts, and this is precisely what Ivan does. The process has value because it holds the mirror up to absurdity. But Ivan's facts become sentimental when he uses them to equate the psychological and the moral, raising both to exemplary abstraction. Dostoevsky's reactionary arguments against the environmental criminologists are based on the premise that moral and spiritual conversion, the most highly individualistic of all education, cannot be predicted, controlled, or described by case histories. Unhampered by novelistic controls, he parallels Ivan's "realism" by depending on the sentimental clichés of Christian abstraction, by fantasizing his own

21. Dostoevsky to Nikolay Nikolayevitch Strachov, Feb. 26, 1869, *Letters*, pp. 166–67. See also Dostoevsky to Apollon Nikolayevitch Maikov, Dec. 11, 1868, *ibid.*, p. 158.

22. For the way in which this adjective passes from tradition to environment, see Donald Fanger, *Dostoevsky and Romantic Realism: A Study of Dostoevsky in Relation to Balzac, Dickens, and Gogol* (Chicago: Univ. of Chicago Press, 1965). The history of Saint Petersburg and its atmosphere are seen through the eyes of Dostoevsky as conducive to and reflective of the kind of abnormality he deals with psychologically.

cases. He speaks of an isolated instance of a Christian doctor's kindness to a Jewish child:

> Were I a painter, I would have painted this "genre," that night at the Jewess' childbed. I am awfully fond of realism in art, but in the pictures of some of our modern realists *there is no moral center,* as a mighty poet and a refined artist expressed himself the other day.

He describes the miserable Jewish shanty and fills out the picture:

> Presently, the tired little old man, turning for a moment from the mother, takes hold of the child; there is nothing to swathe him with; there is even no duster (gentlemen, I swear that such misery exists; it does exist, it's pure realism, realism reaching the level of the fantastic).[23]

The Christian doctor, of course, takes the shirt off his back to wrap up the child. In another instance, after creating a sentimental story of a poor boy frozen on Christmas Eve and taken in by Christ to a heaven of children who had died miserably, Dostoevsky asks:

> And why did I invent such a story, one that conforms so little to an ordinary, reasonable diary—especially a writer's diary? And that, after having promised to write stories pre-eminently about actual events! But the point is that I keep fancying that all this could actually have happened—I mean, the things which happened in the basement and behind the piles of kindling wood. Well, and as regards Christ's Christmas tree—I really don't know what to tell you, and I don't know whether or not this could have happened. Being a novelist, I have to invent things.[24]

The novel's transvaluated realism does not stop at case histories of fantastic facts; it depends on a humbler tension between the psychological and the moral. This tension behind the final scene

23. Dostoevsky, *Diary,* II, 657.
24. *Ibid.,* I, 172.

of cheers for Karamazov marks the difference between the children's moving acceptance and the monolithic abstraction, "Karamazov," of the case for the prosecution. The spiritual precipitates the action and alleviates, but never professes to cancel, the tension in the real world of the humanist's novel.

Some critics have noted a similarity between Dostoevsky's "Alyosha problem" and Milton's "God problem." [25] Since psychology is hell, it is more provocative than the heaven of morality. Because Ivan's psychological complexity, his yearnings contradicting his words, is what makes him interesting, he seems to be in a privileged position. Both Satan and Ivan make themselves more impressive by moralizing others. The world that God and Alyosha allow is, however, more interesting than the one that Ivan and Satan construct. The polemicists live by the reduction of variety. If Alyosha seems less convincing, it is not because he does not recognize the absurd "facts" of our moral degradation, not because he is not angered by them; it is because he refuses to let them dominate and describe the individual case, to legislate sin as the socialists legislate happiness. He is relieved by translating words of judgment into Christian works so that his own density is necessarily thinned. The new Dmitri may not seem as real as the old one, but for the first time he knows by his relationships that he is not fantastic. That our outrage at the miscarriage of justice is considerably soothed by this compensation indicates that the transvaluation has worked on us. We may always have difficulty feeling the Alyosha whom Dostoevsky gives us in this novel, but we are continually moved by the intensity of his desires for others.[26] Alyosha never moralizes personality out of existence. Both

25. See, for example, Eliseo Vivas, "The Two Dimensions of Reality in *The Brothers Karamazov*," in *Creation and Discovery* (Chicago: Regnery, 1955), pp. 71–107.
26. Dostoevsky writes that the Russian people should not be judged "by what they are, but by what they strive to become" (*Diary*, I, 202). In Alyosha's case this use of the ideal for the real can be, as Jackson puts it, "a working ethic for mortals," just as it might become the justification for war outside the novel ("Dmitrij Karamazov," p. 265). An ironically ineffectual display of nonimperialistic idealism is touchingly presented in Dostoevsky's portrait of Stepan Verkhovensky, whose Oblomovitis, being

Dmitri and Alyosha in their tragic gladness take the risks of simplicity and plagiarism, and affirm only in the face of the absurd, only by resistance and repetition, by squandering the self.

When Alyosha kisses Ivan after the story of the Grand Inquisitor, Ivan teases his brother and calls him a plagiarist (I, 309). And though Ivan is delighted at the act, he is, we must imagine, impressed not only by the love but by the effect of the poem. Ivan puts a high value on his literary efforts, though they come back to haunt him (as Dostoevsky continually brags in his letters about his own originality). Ivan is moved by the originality of his indictment, and the reader is far more stimulated by his dialectic than by the poor words of Alyosha. But precisely because Alyosha is a plagiarist, he is not haunted by doubles. While Smerdyakov and Rakitin plagiarize Ivan to murder and reduce, Alyosha borrows to transform the word to acts of love, to lead the self to others. The echoing of Father Zossima's early speech to the women, especially his words to Mrs. Khokhlakov, in Alyosha's final speech to the children (which would have had very little effect had it been uttered at the beginning of the novel), and the repetition of the major refrain "Do not be afraid of life. Do not be afraid of love." typify the way in which word is converted to drama throughout the novel. The backsliding progress of the humanist life that grows with conversation typically deglamorizes the word. Alyosha's plagiarism clears the way for active love, as Ivan's doubled words become only echoes. The fear of life throws up a thousand phrases and formulas. Alyosha deals in pancakes, not in Russian solutions; like Kierkegaard's knight of faith, he is able to "fall down in such a way that the same second it looks as if [he] were standing and walking." He is able "to transform the leap of life into a walk, absolutely to express the sublime in the pedestrian." [27]

---

less willed than Ivan's related disease, allows Dostoevsky to love him more than he ever could Ivan (see *Diary*, I, 379).

27. Kierkegaard, *Fear and Trembling*, in *Fear and Trembling and Sickness unto Death*, p. 52.

[Tolerance] entails imagination. For you have all the time to be putting yourself in someone else's place. Which is a desirable spiritual exercise.

E. M. Forster

The present generation, wearied by its chimerical efforts, relapses into complete indolence. Its condition is that of a man who has only fallen asleep towards morning: first of all come great dreams, then a feeling of laziness, and finally a witty or clever excuse for remaining in bed.

Sören Kierkegaard

After a number of innovations one repeats oneself, for art and wit have their limits. Only God and some few rare geniuses can keep forging ahead into novelty.

Denis Diderot

CHAPTER SIX

The Twentieth-Century Novel:
Old Wine in New Bottles

A SELF-RIGHTEOUS prosecution of most fictional conventions and a confidence in the possibility of finding a form that truly expresses our contemporary reality permeate the pages of Nathalie Sarraute's *Era of Suspicion*. It is the tone of the absurdist.[1] The criticisms and recommendations of France's "new" novelists, who describe the intentions and feelings of many practitioners of fiction, reveal some of the reasons why the novel's humanism is having such a difficult critical time. The absurdist scene, character, and style, a literature of extreme reaction motivated by a suspicion of the old personality and all its trappings, is a presence that can hardly be ignored. Nor can the discomfort that novelists like Norman Mailer feel about the relation of fiction to current events be disregarded. In the second part of *Armies of the Night* Mailer deliberately reduces his novel to history and puts it to use as a collective record. Such a strategy illustrates a self-consciousness about fiction's relation to a history that does not seem to want to listen to it. The humor of the defensive and vulnerable self seems shamed

1. Nathalie Sarraute concludes an article on Flaubert by terming the novelist, despite important qualifications, a herald of the "new novel." See "Flaubert," *Partisan Review*, XXXIII, no. 2 (1966), 194–208.

by the call to political purpose. The present appears to have no time for the play of the complex and conservative novelist of the first part of his book. It is significant that the novel half has all the time in the world to play with the times. Mailer himself is rather touchingly amazed at his abrupt radicalism in newspaper and television interviews, and his novel turned history surprises him by climaxing in the apocalyptic "metaphor delivered," in which the personality of Mailer as character finally dissolves. Mailer the outraged citizen finds himself impatient with the ineffectual lives of poets and friends, with the negative capability of the merely sympathetic eye. Yet Mailer the novelist is aware that the uses of the novel derive from the ways in which it cannot conquer history, cannot organize it and cannot cap or lead it. He knows that we read his novel for the faces he draws, not for the souls he delivers.

It is easy to underrate the flexibility of humanism. But humanism, as it can work with any shape of history, can work with forms favored by the contemporary sensibility—confession, satanic debate, and parody—and can turn them to its own uses. When these forms frame the humanist attitude they set up a friction that often delights us by the surprises of reverse expectation. That the humanist so easily goes beyond these forms is an effective and implicit criticism of the limitations imposed on them by an absurdist imagination anxious to save itself by and for art. As Gide infers by his citation of this Vauvenargues epigram in "The Journal of *The Counterfeiters*," "Those who do not get outside of themselves are all of a piece." [2] The humanist's deployment of imagination into independent characters, his "anti-egoistic force of decentralization," as Gide's Edouard calls it, takes us back to Montaigne, whose rhythms are quite marked in many of Edouard's statements, and to his gentle deritualizing of confession. The novelist who discovers his life by giving it away in "procurations

2. André Gide, "The Journal of *The Counterfeiters*," trans. Justin O'Brien, in *The Counterfeiters*, trans. Dorothy Bussy (New York: Random House, 1927), p. 451.

and espousals" could not have a self defined merely by its justification.[3]

The old antithesis between Montaigne and Rousseau underlies that between Edouard and Passavant/Strouvilhou; it is the antithesis between Edouard's relaxed claim that "nothing could be more different from me than myself" and Rousseau's boast of wit that "I am at least different from others." The humanist is continually startled, not by the higher truth of his lying, but by the way his creations keep him from claiming his fiction as truth. Gide translates the classical and Christian spending of the self into the aesthetic illusion of characters who seem to choose their own communicative form. The author who cannot get past doubles of his own mind is determined by his own needs. Gide speaks of this distinction as he muses on the limitations of *Si le grain ne meurt:*

> Even while writing it I was led to think that intimacy, insight, psychological investigation can in certain respects be carried even further in the "novel" than in "confessions." In the latter, one is sometimes hampered by the "I"; there are some complexities one cannot try to disentangle, to expose without seeming self-centered. Everything I have seen, everything I have learned, everything that has happened to me for several months, I should like to get into this novel, where it will serve to enrich the texture. I should like events never to be related directly by the author, but instead exposed (and several times from different vantages) by those actors who will be influenced by those events. In their account of the action, I should like the events to appear slightly warped; the reader will take a sort of interest from the mere fact of having to *reconstruct*. The story requires his collaboration to take shape properly.[4]

The proper reconstruction is of course counterfeit, but the collaboration of limited selves leads to a mutual examination of the fictions of our own consciousness. The hero of events catches up with us, as Bernard journeys from literature to life, from analysis

3. Gide, *Counterfeiters*, p. 71.
4. Gide, "Journal of *The Counterfeiters*," pp. 415–16.

and allusion to instinct and spontaneity, paralleling the artist's dying into life. (This complicity is very different from the reconstruction that such "new" novelists as Alain Robbe-Grillet demand from their readers; our task in the new novel leads us no closer to a sympathy with others.) The humanist's pretense is the apparent unpredictability of the novel's course:

> X. maintains that a good novelist, before he begins to write his book, ought to know how it is going to finish. As for me, who let mine flow where it will, I consider that life never presents us with anything which may not be looked upon as a fresh starting point, no less than as a termination. "Might be continued"—these are my words which I should like to finish my *Counterfeiters*.[5]

In such a way, through the imperfect vision of Edouard, does Gide pay honor to Montaigne, and in such a way the humanist novelist is free to incorporate absurdist forms as well as any other contemporary expression of reality.

Confession

A deliberately one-sided monologue, while it may not confine our aesthetic vision, forces us to go outside the work to find our measure. The exclusively absurdist tone jars our sensibilities:

> But I feel sure that you are again imagining that I am joking. Or perhaps it's just the contrary, and you are convinced that I really think so. Anyway, gentlemen, I shall welcome both views as an honor and a special favor. And do forgive my digression.[6]

By this wit, the underground man pushes us away. And, in Camus's *The Fall*, Jean-Baptiste Clamence's confession "I earned my

5. Gide, *Counterfeiters*, p. 335.
6. Dostoevsky, *Notes from Underground*, ed. and trans. Ralph Matlaw (New York: E. P. Dutton, 1960), p. 42.

living by carrying on a dialogue with people I scorned" is hardly made more bearable by his acts as converted judge-penitent.[7] Both Clamence and the underground man give us an honesty and wisdom that we might admire did we not feel violated by their buttonholing. Both are, after all, willing to admit that "authors of confession write to avoid confessing."[8] Both are aware that the final truth, known only by the confessor, is a strategy of justification and an excuse for prosecution. The self-indulgence of both confessors is evident. It is that of the man who has "never felt comfortable except in lofty places"[9] or in mouseholes, the man who ultimately uses self-judgment as a license to judge others. The extremes of masochistic reversals sanction a special consciousness, a consciousness so afraid of life that it historicizes human relationships into eternal questions.

Ironically, a pertinent critic of these two penitent judges is Kafka, who writes:

> One of the most senseless things in this wide world is the serious treatment of the problem of guilt, at least so it seems to me. It's not the uttering of reproaches that seems to me senseless; certainly when one is in distress, one utters reproaches in all directions. . . . It's also comprehensible that one takes such reproaches to heart at a time of agitation and turmoil; but that one should consider it possible to argue about it as about any ordinary arithmetical problem which is so clear that it produces results for daily conduct, this I don't understand at all. Of course, you are to blame, but then your husband is also to blame and then you again in the living together of human beings and the blame piles up in endless succession until it reaches the grey Original Sin, but what use can it be for my present day or for the visit to the doctor in Ischl to rummage about in eternal sin?[10]

7. Albert Camus, *The Fall*, trans. Justin O'Brien (New York: Knopf, 1959), p. 18.
8. *Ibid.*, p. 120.
9. *Ibid.*, p. 23.
10. Franz Kafka, *Letters to Milena*, trans. Tania and James Stern, ed. Willi Haas (New York: Schocken, 1953), p. 193.

Alyosha insists on telling Ivan that he is not guilty since no man is innocent. The terror of judgment stems from the inability to accept a secular grace, the forgiveness of the self. The humoring of guilt clears the way for a tempering of the absurd confession that absorbs the form within the novel itself.

The tone of *The Confessions of Zeno*, like that of Montaigne, subjects the confession to an appealing alchemy. The illusion of a spontaneous back talk of character to authorial control is registered through Zeno's continual capacity to be surprised into self-perception by alien lives. Zeno is, like the underground man or the Beckett hero, a compulsive talker. But, while the absurdist's extreme verbal poses are a strategy of self-preservation, for Zeno talking is something else. When the young Ada directly and simply tells of her experience in England, he admits:

> I liked her simple way of talking all the more because I myself could not open my mouth without misrepresenting things or people, for otherwise I should have seen no use in talking at all. Talking seemed to me an event in itself which must not be hampered by any other events.[11]

His flippancy might seem to align him with the fantastic Fyodor Karamazov, who is intensely interested in making himself felt as a clown, but in fact Zeno's confession ardently courts a world of varying consciousness and loves, honors, and obeys it.

Svevo's entire novel takes us to the heart of the novel's humanism by asserting that conversation has values not to be sacrificed on the altar of truth. A mournful Kafka reveals a resentment of the Zenos who keep muddying literature with life:

> I hate everything that does not relate to literature, conversations bore me (even if they relate to literature), to visit people bores me, the sorrows, the joys of my relatives bore me to my soul.

11. Italo Svevo, *The Confessions of Zeno*, trans. Beryl de Zoete (New York: Knopf, 1958), p. 68. Future references will be to this edition and will be noted in the text.

Conversations take the importance, the seriousness, the truth out of everything, I think.[12]

One of the deepest absurdist beliefs is here exposed—that one can reach the truth only by overriding or dissolving the characters who act it out and spoil it. In the face of what he interprets as psychoanalysis's expectation of uncovering the one and only genuine history, Zeno calls his remembrances lies, "invention," "creative act" (p. 368). Were he an absurdist, he might glory in the inescapable historical betrayal of human hopes and make his idealized thrust toward a future purification. But he does not. His sense of self-irony prevents it. He makes a critical discovery at the end of the *Confessions* when he realizes that the re-creating memory, trying for authenticity, is forever stamped with the personality of the present evoker. In his comedy, Zeno makes his analyst a fool so that he can be his own doctor:

> I was bathed in perspiration while creating the images, and in tears when I recognized them. The idea of being able to live again one day of innocence and inexperience gave me inexpressible delight. . . . Was it not like the miracle of plucking in October the roses of May? (p. 368).

He as last "overtakes" his "memory-pictures" and at that moment realizes that he invented them. Invention fills the mind with situations and faces that have the "solidity, the color, and the movement of living things" (p. 368). The recognition that memory is fiction need not reduce its work to indolent and solipsistic daydreaming. If the patient is in fact not literally evoking his childhood, he is feeling its presence and its relationship to all those figures that have surrounded him. The invention is a provisional act, and the density of experience remembered is a provisional wealth:

12. Kafka, *The Diaries of Franz Kafka*, trans. Joseph Kresh, ed. Max Brod (London: Schocken, 1948), I, 292.

The sun! the sun! dazzling sunlight! From the picture of what I thought to be my youth, so much sun streamed out that it was hard for me not to believe in it (p. 371).

The cure, declared on the assumption that these recollections can exorcise the obsessive patterns that have structured the novel in mock psychiatric form, is to Zeno, creator of fictions and lover of conversations, absurd. Despite his complaints about the habit of memory, these faces, as they turn toward him in reproach or tenderness and as they spread through the novel, authenticate Zeno himself. It is significant that his final apocalyptic vision of the earth's destruction, though convincing and horrifying, is ultimately irrelevant to this truth. Zeno is interested only in being sufficient unto the day and its diseases. His humor pushes him back to life's business of profits and losses. It follows the line of Ada's ailment, Basedow's disease, with its "goiter at one end and a dropsy at the other . . . and all along the line, throughout the whole of humanity there is no such thing as perfect health" (p. 287).

Zeno's explorations, which lead him to the world's affairs, would push the absurdist to his bed. Beckett's unnamable complains:

> All this business of a labor to accomplish, before I can end, of an imposed task, once known, long neglected, finally forgotten, to perform, before I can be done with speaking, done listening, I invented it all, in the hope it would console me, help me to go on a road, moving, between a beginning and an end, gaining ground, losing ground, getting lost, but somehow in the long run making headway. All lies. I have nothing to do, that is to say nothing in particular. I have to speak, whatever that means.[13]

He cannot adjust to experience's inventions. The job of living is historicized. Zeno can tolerate the fictionality of purposes without despair. It is enough to know that "it is essential to keep moving" (p. 287), lest, like Rilke's Nikolai Kusmitch, one get dizzy from

---

13. Samuel Beckett, *The Unnamable*, in *Three Novels by Samuel Beckett* (New York: Grove, 1965), p. 314.

the earth's spinning and be forced to lie down for the rest of one's days.[14] "Life," says Zeno, "has its poisons, but counter-poisons too which balance them. It is only by moving about that one can avoid the first and profit by the second" (p. 287). Dancing on the line is a refusal to take life lying down; for Zeno, he who retreats to the couch—whether it be the couch of analysis, Ivan's bed of philosophical nails, Stepan Verkhovensky's sofa of the true and beautiful, the languid bed of Oblomovitis, or Beckett's bed of babble—is poisoned by truth and suffers from "perfect health" or the desire for it, which becomes perfect sickness, a purity to will one thing.

Kafka, the most vulnerable and attractive hibernator, gives us by his own example an interesting analysis of the relation between the humanist novel and the bedroom drama of retreat. In the second volume of his *Diaries*, which is studded with visions, masks, and doubles, he writes:

> What will be my fate as a writer is very simple. My talent for portraying my dreamlike inner life has thrust all other matters into the background; my life has dwindled dreadfully, nor will it cease to dwindle. Nothing else will ever satisfy me. But the strength I can muster for that portrayal is not to be counted upon: perhaps it has already vanished forever, perhaps it will come back to me again, although the circumstances of my life don't favor its return. Thus I waver, continually fly to the summit of the mountain, but then fall back in a moment.[15]

We recognize the absurdist's lament. The vampirism of the sacred-font relationship between life and art takes place behind closed doors. Kafka complains:

> Yesterday evening, already with a sense of foreboding, pulled the cover off the bed, lay down and again became aware of all my abilities as though I were holding them in my hand; they tightened my chest, they set my head on fire; for a short while,

---

14. Rainer Rilke, *The Notebooks of Malte Laurids Brigge*, trans. Norton M. Herter (New York: Norton, 1949), pp. 151–52.

15. Kafka, *Diaries*, II, 77.

to console myself for not getting up to work, I repeated: "That's not healthy, that's not healthy," and with almost visible purpose tried to draw sleep over my head. I kept thinking of a cap with a visor which, to protect myself, I pulled down hard over my forehead. How much did I lose yesterday, how the blood pounded in my tight head, capable of anything and restrained only by powers which are indispensable for my very life and are here being wasted.[16]

Here is no comfort, only fate. The expense of spirit in the sickness of superior consciousness is described by Nietzsche, who speaks of those who climb the mountains of the bedroom:

> To be ill is a sort of resentment in itself. Against this resentment the invalid has only one great remedy—I call it *Russian fatalism*, that fatalism which is free from revolt, and with which the Russian soldier, to whom a campaign proves unbearable, ultimately lays himself down in the snow.[17]

Zeno refuses to desocialize his hypochondriacal afflictions. He insists, through conversation, in living them with others. His small resentments measure, not his denial of life, but his need for more of it than he feels he has. The retraction of identity for fear of its disintegration represents in Beckett's unnamable the extreme form of "Russian fatalism," which assumes that the body is "condemned to life" while the mind cannot endure the assumption.[18] The synthetic voice of the novel registers the inevitable and ultimate irony that "to decompose is to live too."[19] For Zeno this realization is finally a source of relief, since the poison of death is countered by emetics of rebirth, all in a day's work. Without a name or face, the final amalgam of Beckett's voices dissolves the tension between ideas of order and the day's decay. This tension is the source of the absurdist's dramatic coherence, as in Flaubert and

16. *Ibid.*, I, 151.
17. Nietzsche, "Ecce Homo," in *The Philosophy of Nietzsche*, trans. Oscar Levy, ed. Geoffrey Clive (New York: New American Library, 1965), pp. 44–45.
18. Beckett, *The Unnamable*, p. 325.
19. Beckett, *Molloy*, in *Three Novels*, p. 25.

Proust, and when it goes, there are no supporting fictions left.[20] The unnamable's repetitive monologues keep him not only from hearing the voices of his neighbors, but also from using his own voice to humor theirs. The voices of others prevent Zeno from ever honoring the illusion that art is superior to life.

The fable contest between Guido and Zeno shows how successfully the unpredictable personality can pierce the armor of pattern and form. Guido says of Zeno's second fable, "It is not a fable, it is only an excuse for calling me a fool"; Zeno laughs, "and the pain that had inspired [him] to write it at once vanished" (p. 280). No laughter, no recognition could send the underground man out of the room back into the world, but business cures Zeno; his confession, because he invites his reader and the other characters to take advantage of him, helps him to socialize his lies and thus endure them.

Again and again Zeno voices absurdist protests and takes absurdist stances only to overturn them by his self-irony. Thus, his hypochondria expresses his desire for innocence: "I rebelled at last against my own sense of guilt, for I was innocent and had nothing to hide" (p. 276). Yet, like his confession, his protest is not a way of separating himself from the world; on the contrary, it is an admission of his need to be loved. He does not make of the tension between the old morality (life is good or bad) and his discovery that life is original (p. 299) an excuse for disdain and a license for an autonomous ethic. On the contrary, the irresistibility of Zeno's humor is that all his discoveries, even those that precede analysis, are continually upset by life, as habit defeats all resolutions. Intellectually he plays games with the limitations of Augusta's moral

20. In an interesting review of Beckett, Leo Bersani writes: "The fear of losing the self in its roles is—as Beckett must have realized in his study of Proust—a fear of losing the self in time. And the illusion of a self outside of time is a retreat not only from life, but also from literature, a retreat, that is, from the uncertain futures to which time and language subject both the self and books. Beckett's extreme attempt to render literature autonomous is an ironic reminder of the ultimate dependence of literature on life" ("No Exit for Beckett," *Partisan Review*, XXXIII, no. 2 [1966], p. 267).

consolations. He mocks the ease of her religion and the hermetic nature of her health. But the most touching comedy of the novel occurs when Zeno lets Augusta defeat his superiority with unreflective acts of love. Thus, his aristocratic anguish and consciousness are intellectually asserted: "Health cannot analyze itself even if it looks at itself in the glass. It is only we invalids who can know anything about ourselves" (p. 146). Then, devoured by fears of death, he wants Augusta to comfort him; he asks her by giving himself mock pity: "Poor Cosini." What follows is one of many superb bits of compassionate humor in which all his wit is tamed:

> So I always succeeded in being comforted by her even when the cause of my distress was quite different. One day, when I was feeling quite ill at the thought of having been unfaithful to her, I murmured by mistake: "Poor Cosini." I was glad that I had, for it was infinitely sweet to be comforted by her even in a case like that (pp. 147–48).

Such a spirit keeps him from being a superfluous man.

No one could be more unlike the targets of the underground man than Zeno's rival, Guido. His initial presence recalls strongly the absurdist's competitive and superior double, who wins in love, words, and music. But by self-mockery Zeno reverses the usual pattern of victimization. Even after Guido's death Zeno gains no victory, for Guido had gained none over him. When Ada, about to leave his life, reproaches him for not having loved Guido enough, though the concept of life's originality should relieve him of guilt, Zeno replays the frustration he felt at his father's death: "The tears blinded my eyes. She was leaving us forever. Never again should I be able to prove to her that I was innocent" (p. 365). Morality and psychology remain in tension, resisting the possibility of dissolution in the mind of the humanist. Life cures Zeno of the need for the meaning of life, for life refuses to follow principle. He accepts comedy's competition and plays hard at it. Kafka, on the other hand, obsessively fears "connection, . . . passing into the other. Then," he worries, "I'll never be alone again." [21] This is the anxiety for which Dostoevsky punishes Ivan and for which, in a contemporary version of Ivan's debate with his devil, Bellow's Allbee tortures the frightened Leventhal.

Satanic Debate

The great eternal questions of Ivan's Russia offered an escape from the world's brothers, but for those who recognize and maintain, "in contrast to the metaphysicians, . . . many *mortal* souls" within them,[22] the devil's doubling of the self is played out in secular comedy and the question of guilt is socialized. This comedy, developed in an absurd tradition (which includes Dostoevsky's *The Double* and "The Eternal Husband"), features Gogolian solutions for victims of madness, fantasy, or death. But the humanist must come back into the world; his comedy is supported by Kafka's very practical question "What use can it be for my present day . . . to rummage about in eternal sin?" [23] It is this worldly acceptance that backs up the last scene of Bellow's *The Victim*. Leventhal cries out to Allbee, "Wait a minute, what's your idea of who runs things?" The unanswered question, present throughout the novel, is finally anticlimactic as Leventhal steps down from the absurdist stage:

> But he heard Mary's voice at his back. Allbee ran in and sprang up the stairs. The bell continued its dinning, and Leventhal and Mary were still in the aisle when the houselights went off. An usher showed them to their seats.[24]

Ivan's devil assumes the threadbare pose and wit of the Enlightenment, plagiarizes Goethe's Mephistopheles, and yearns for secu-

21. Kafka, *Diaries*, I, 292.
22. Nietzsche, "Human All Too Human," in *Philosophy*, p. 245.
23. Kafka, *Letters to Milena*, p. 193.
24. Saul Bellow, *The Victim* (New York: Vanguard, 1956), p. 294. Future references will be to this edition and will be noted in the text.

lar security in the body of a merchant's wife. But with the unjudg-
ing and silent presence of Christ in the wings, the debate between
Ivan and his devil is put in its proper place in the hierarchical scale
of values. The devil's domestication and social glibness are meant
to be reflections of the enlightened absurdity of Ivan's demands
and expectations. Social solutions to metaphysical anguish, justice
as a balm for guilt, give birth to a pathetic and witty double-dealer
instead of a great vision of evil who can justify a retreat to the
wilderness. The unreality of Ivan's solutions is symbolized by his
double's anachronistic costume of superfluity. When Bellow
comes to the universe's greatest debate between the soul and the
devil he does not have the backdrop of spiritual relief. Like Svevo,
he takes an absurdist structure, substituting for confession the
isolated and staged philosophical confrontation, and makes of it
a humanist novel. And he does this without turning the "old"
dialogue to farce. His comedy uses it seriously.

Like Dr. Rieux, hero of Camus's *The Plague*, Leventhal ultimately realizes that to be merely human, neither more nor less,
is the most difficult and necessary role. That he is initially less
than human is attested to by the sudden appearance of a double.
"Nice people," says Golyadkin's servant in *The Double*, "don't
live falsely and don't have doubles." [25] Only fantastic people do.
And Leventhal is, for all his conventionality, fantastic for the
usual reasons: an absence of living fathers, an absence of living
brothers, and an assumption that his own determinism can be a
mode of self-preservation. His devil, Allbee, confronts him to
expose this assumption. Fate, which is at the beginning a most
serious matter but always in somebody else's hands, is left hang-
ing at the end of the book. In the course of the novel, Leventhal
must face the curse of assimilation, made certain and easy by the
disappearance of Messiah and fathers.[26] Flushed out of his burrow,

25. Dostoevsky, *The Double*, trans. George Bird (Bloomington: Indiana
Univ. Press, 1958), p. 157.
26. The Messiah has become a parlor joke to the secular Jew (see pp.
253–54).

without metaphysical or ghetto security, he is stripped to an existential base and must shop for suitable clothing.

The fathers were presumably luckier. Their roles, which had pragmatic as well as psychological advantages, helped them to survive: "Ruf mir Yoshke, ruf mir Moshke, / Aber gib mir die groschke" (p. 111). The old script, the old refrain, made acting convincing. And the old costumes fit well on stage. Leventhal's father had the comfort of great and consistent enemies whose composition was never questioned. He knew how to take advantage of abstraction. The enemy could never be disproved if he could not be lived with. But the costumes of the fathers no longer fit the sons; on stage they make men clowns. Leventhal's pantomime of anonymity is suddenly threatened by a melodramatic demonstration of harlequinism in which talk substitutes for deed, paranoiac threats for camaraderie. His evocation of roles by Allbee's own adaptation of victimization is the first step in a therapy of extremes that, when exhausted, will enable the two to survive their stripping. When the debate subsides, the doubles get down from the stage to take their seats in the audience.

As the demonstration of absurdist escapes and demands ("Am I my brother's keeper?" "Who runs things?") cools, it rebuilds into conversation. Allbee's last biblical retort, "Increase and multiply," becomes a fond reminder of a relationship:

> It seemed to him that Allbee had no real desire to be malicious; he was merely obedient to habit. He might have been smiling at himself and making an appeal of a sort from understanding (p. 292).

Leventhal finally realizes that the demand for justice, the need for self-justification, the compulsion to blame—all mirrored in Allbee's paranoiac face—arose from an error,

> a conviction or illusion that at the start of life, and perhaps even before, a promise had been made. In thinking of this promise,

Leventhal compared it to a ticket, a theater ticket. And with his ticket, a man entitled to an average seat might feel too shabby for the dress circle or sit in it defiantly and arrogantly; another, entitled to the best in the house, might cry out in rage to the usher who led him to the third balcony (p. 286).

The illusion is not eradicated, but Leventhal no longer allows it to paralyze him. Ivan insists on a better ticket, but his demands are not so different from those of the imagined complainers about life's luck. Like the Ur-promise, concepts of the promised children of God or the Promised Land—assumptions that Allbee mocks—reinforce the victim psychology. But if there need be no victims by metaphysical fiat, neither are any required by specifically assumed social composition. Leventhal is revealed as victimized only as long as he fails to realize his humanity.

To strip off the excuses of historicizing, Bellow sets the representative "promised" on stage. The purity of situation will have to be overcome both structurally and thematically as the aesthetic and moral directions share the drama of self-irony. The dialogue begins in the best satanic tradition, with the question of the devil's reality:

> ALLBEE: Well, now you've found out that I still exist and you're going home, is that it? . . .
> LEVENTHAL: Why should I doubt that you exist? (p. 29).[27]

Allbee, like Ivan's devil, has been mysteriously called to the nightmare: "Of course, you're pretending you didn't get the letter." He confirms the comedy of doubles by answering Leventhal's "What, are we related?" with a comic denial of Jewish kinship, "By blood? No, no . . . heavens." The implications are clear from the beginning that the drama is fantastic because the lives being examined are historicized. They have a common base of retreat from the responsibility of being merely human. The dia-

---

27. We might keep in mind not only Ivan's devil, but Gide's projected spirit in "Journal of *The Counterfeiters*," who asks: "Why should you be afraid of me? You know very well I don't exist" (p. 467).

logue of self-preservation is pushed through farce so that Leventhal can eventually join us off stage.

Somewhere between Bellow's metaphorically established boundaries, between Disraeli the Jewish "clown" of history and Caliban the contaminator of tradition, between historical elevation and biological reduction, between hoarding and spending, is the unglamorous, merely human role. Allbee overacts to find the balance, and Leventhal is forced into his drama. The insanity of hiding between cultural stereotypes is exposed by the light of an exorcistic farce. "Sometimes I feel . . . as if I were in a sort of Egyptian darkness. You know, Moses punished the Egyptians with darkness" (p. 144), says Allbee in one stab; in another, "But I go into the library once in a while to look around, and last week I saw a book about Thoreau and Emerson by a man named Lipschitz" (p. 145). The enemy—the promised people or the despoilers—no longer give relief. Allbee and Leventhal, almost in spite of themselves, are compelled to act out and support all the clichés from Jewish guilt to Anglo-Saxon drunkenness, and they must do so without an audience. (Leventhal is never domesticated with the other characters in the novel while his secret melodrama is going on at home.) Leventhal is hotly uncharitable to anyone who translates the frustration of role-calling and slander directed against oneself into overcompensating acts. He criticizes the overacting of Disraeli, who by reversing stereotype assumed it and made of history a personal test that turned it into a merely vulgar surprise. He criticizes the overacting of Allbee, too, who so often seems unreal. Both cases beam back the revelation that Leventhal, unwilling to forgo stereotype, has been consistently underacting, and that good acting, spoken extemporaneously, is "what is exactly human" (p. 133). The slave morality of resentment and the slave psychology of paranoia are recited on stage in the slave vocabulary of victim and victimizer. Leventhal has yet to understand that the ability to surmount humiliating roles is the ticket to humanism.

The novel's epigraph from *1001 Nights* suggests that responsibility is both absurd and necessary, a commitment superior to the illusion of innocence. Allbee identifies Leventhal's hoarding of spirit as a "Jewish point of view" that says, with Job's counselors, you must deserve what you get and my hands are clean (p. 146). Allbee has behind him all the absurd leaps of love demonstrated by Christ. As soon as Leventhal adopts the collective reference, a strange thing happens. He is trapped into using Allbee's style and says: "Millions of us have been killed. What about that?" (p. 147). He is forced to see through his victimization because he has fallen for abstraction, the line of least resistance. When he hears himself saying this kind of thing he realizes how relevant Allbee is to him, how real. Before this realization, he regrets not failures of understanding but his inability to disregard Allbee. He comforts himself with the vocabulary of the riot squad: "Hit them! That was all they understood" (p. 148). And he is more concerned with his dignity than with his human failure when he tells himself: "You couldn't say you were master of yourself when there were so many people by whom you could be humiliated" (p. 149). He even toys with an admiration of his father's philosophy of "getting one's due," which is the very claim he despises as psychological cliché in Allbee. But, after recognizing Allbee's reality, he never again manages to believe that as a stereotype he deserves to be set apart from his vulgar double. The hoarder and the waster are doomed to march past each other on the ledge of purgatory; as they pass, their silhouettes merge.

Leventhal's attempt to find out if he literally is obligated to Allbee is a travesty of Allbee's cry from the heart. The words that Allbee so cleverly manipulates trap Leventhal and keep him from seeking the spirit behind them. But he is a victim only because he chooses to take Allbee at his word. His generosity to his brother's family, an emblem of Jewish concern, is a token fulfillment of duty and therefore suspect. He scrupulously follows through to the letter of caricature, and his acting is no more convincing to him than are his accusations against Allbee. Consequently, he is filled with misgivings and is desirous of vindication. His rite of passage is from a literal innocence that insists that two plus two are four to a recognition that proof is as irrelevant to a judgment of complicity as logic is to love. In the end, the drama walks off stage. Being human is a difficult role to perform night after night. The willingness to live with this repetition is the cornerstone of the humanism that works its truth through fiction.[28]

Parody

Irving Howe and Richard Poirier, among others, have recently been concerned with distinctions between the old and the new modes and tempers of parody in the novel, and there is general agreement that the new relies on the possibility of art itself rather than on the criticism of a tradition.[29] Both absurdists and humanists have been affected, and yet their intentions and uses are crucially different. The humanist refuses to release even the parodic novel from its commitment to human personality and character. The absurdist, indifferent to the psychological demands of others, feels liberated from inclusion in the educative process of mutual exploration; this allows him to display an inventive and unburdened wit and a manipulative agility in the service of epistemology. The wit and intelligence of John Barth seem infinitely free to play with mechanics, plot, history, incident, and style. But the price of decontamination from the world is often a redundant and implosive imagination. Each novelty, released from the bounds of mere experience, can take us in but once; the absurdist's wit is tarnished by self-plagiarism. He uses parody to

28. This is a theme and a metaphor that Bellow explores deeply and with compassionate irony in *Mr. Sammler's Planet* (New York: Viking, 1970), his finest tribute to the ardors of humanism.

29. See Irving Howe, "The Culture of Modernism," *Commentary*, XLIV, no. 5 (1967), 48–59; and Richard Poirier, "The Politics of Self-Parody," *Partisan Review*, XXXV, no. 3 (1968), 339–53.

spring himself from moral and aesthetic commitments or expectations, while the humanist uses parody in the same way that he uses history—in the service, not the mastery, of contemporary life. We have become familiar with the unchallenged ways of parodic freedom that shout, "Look at these fictions!" This celibate freedom is only hampered by sympathy and therefore wants to steer clear of it. The absurdist will not let his characters get their hooks in him, nor will he give them the opportunity to diminish him. He saves his identity by outwitting them.

In a novel like Barth's *The Sot-Weed Factor* history and literature and their pretenses of truth are teased, but the process of transvaluation never translates the epistemological problem into a moral one. Character is exhausted for the sake of the artistic imagination, and Barth parodies history in order to historicize his imagination. The black humor of the absurdist parody reveals human limitations so that the authorial mind can escape from them with his creation. If readers of Barth and Beckett often testify only to a bored admiration, it is because they feel excluded from the exercises of wit, which are almost antithetical to Forster's "spiritual exercise" of tolerance that demands "putting yourself in someone else's place."

Nothing could be further in direction from Barth's exuberant parodies of counterfeit philosophies, histories, and forms than the parody of these in Gide's *Counterfeiters*. Gide's parody protests the ritualizing of literature, a formality by which the authorial imagination, sacrificing characters and their spontaneous thoughts, can conquer the threat of the alien imagination. Kierkegaard's exposure of the mystic who "chooses himself abstractly" reveals as well the absurdist who is interested in putting on stage the faceless question "Who runs things?":

> One can therefore say that he constantly chooses himself out of the world. But the consequence is that he is unable to choose himself back again into the world.[30]

30. Kierkegaard, *Either/Or*, trans. D. F. and L. M. Swenson (Princeton: Princeton Univ. Press, 1949), II, p. 208. The discussion of the mystic's psychology appears on pp. 202, 207.

This movement contrasts with the will to yoke spirit to situation, "wherewith at the very same instant I choose myself out of the world I am choosing myself back into the world." By taking himself out of the world, the absurdist is taken in by himself. Councilor William recognizes the egoistic force of centralization at work: "The individual did not in fact create the world and so does not need to take it so much to heart if the world turns out to be vanity." [31]

That literature, like all our institutions and rationalizations, is counterfeit is no matter for despair. On the contrary, this recognition of absurdity helps the humanist to remain merely human since he is aware of the lies of life and of his own pretense. He refuses to jump over the times that test his humanity. But the absurdist reasons with the mystic, who is described again by Kierkegaard:

> Just as he misunderstood reality and construed it metaphysically as vanity, so, too, he misunderstands the historical and construes it metaphysically as unprofitable labor. The highest significance he can ascribe to the temporal is that it is a time of probation in which again and again one is put to the test without anything really resulting from it and without the individual getting further than he was at the beginning. [32]

Is it any wonder that literature becomes ritual? If personality is deemed vanity, we are protected from its surprises. And certainly no reader will be allowed to share the unexpected with the aesthetic mystic. The New Testament paradox of losing the soul to save it, so dear to Gide and Dostoevsky, gives us the form of the humanist's masquerade: he fictionalizes himself to stay real.

The humanist transvaluates within a world of lies. The absurdist, tortured by this world, cannot get beyond the shock that it is not true; he devises perspectives of pasts and futures, histories and fantasies, the fields of the galloping imagination, in order to

31. *Ibid.*, p. 208.
32. *Ibid.*, p. 209.

keep the imagination untested by this life. Gide's parody, because it includes him, reflects his own authentic counterfeiting. His limitations become part of his drama and are recorded in *The Counterfeiters* by the implicit admission that he is no Dostoevsky, no Fielding, while he uses their styles and tones. The undermining of the self, like the rejection of "surface interest" in style,[33] assures us that his literature is our handmaiden, not our religion; it is an agent for relating and remembering, not merely of creation in itself.

Parody in the contemporary absurdist novel is a serious matter. It clears the way for the heroism of language. The old character, morality, and metaphysics are mere shadows with which substantially fleshed words can box. The maker of metaphors is, like Barth's Burlingame, master of infinite disguises, and this lying, like Kierkegaard's, is meant to deceive us into the one truth— that fiction is a holy compensation for the loss of consoling gods. The novelist as hero uses his words to parody social relationships or spiritual yearnings, not as much in scorn of moral or metaphysical seriousness as in protest against aesthetic limitations. When Stanley Elkin's bad man, conceived as a cluster of rhetorical attributes and actually a parody of a bad man (the moral competition between good and bad is simply the deck of cards) is in solitary confinement in a fantastically stylized prison, he meditates:

> He had been oppressed by the prison's deflecting forms. Even in his resistance to those forms he had been deflected, his life eaten up by a concern with behaviour, the appearance of behaviour. All rights wrested their existence from something inimical to rights. Upstairs, the simplest thing he could will had to be meshed with the prison's routine opposition to the thing willed. This was why he assumed there would be something he could resist in solitary, because he felt his life changed. Upstairs, it was the prison which resisted. Each thing he wanted—*each thing*—the prison did not want. It should have been a relief, then, to get away from the rules of silence, permission slips,

33. Gide, "Journal of *The Counterfeiters*," p. 442.

warden's flags, assigned tables, assemblies, the censuses when the prisoners froze and the pencil man came by to count them. But it wasn't. . . . How could he be Feldman if there was no one to be Feldman to? [34]

The "routine opposition to the thing willed," which was the resistance of the supporting cast of others in the moral and meta-physical novel, and which, in Feldman's post-metaphysical day must be memorized rather than inherited, becomes with Feld-man's "reintegration" an unpredictable rhetorical competition. There is certainly no question of learning or transcending in any of the predetermined postures. In fact, the physiognomy of the prison's crowd is deliberately anonymous. It merely labels what Feldman already has put together:

> What a place, he thought. Thieves, he thought, safe-crackers, bookies, guys who jump cars. Pickpockets, he thought. Larcen-ists and arsonists and murderers in all degrees. Rapers, em-bezzlers, hit-and-run drivers. Fences and inciters to riot. Bag-men, wheelmen, fixers and bribers. Kidnappers, he thought, counterfeiters, short-changers, pushers and pimps. Menslaugh-terers, drunken drivers, and guys who didn't give fair measure. Jack-offs. Disturbers of the peace. Vandals. Scoff laws. Bad sports (p. 63).

The crowd of words reflects and predicts that Feldman's vision of self is only a grab bag of words:

> He had it in him, he felt, to be a favorite, like a fatty, like a baldy, like a loony, like a spoony. Like a dummy. Like a guy with clap, with lush, beautiful daughters, with a small dong. He envied the loved, classic fall guys and thought with jealousy of the libeled butts in the prison paper: the "Nigger Lips" Johnsons and "Pigface" Parkers and "Beergut" Kellys and all the others.
>
> "Give me gland trouble," he prayed. "Treble my chins and pull back my hairline. Make me a farter, a stutterer, a guy bad at games. A patsy make me. Amen" (p. 152).

34. Stanley Elkin, *A Bad Man* (New York: Random House, 1967), p. 127. Future references will be to this edition and will be noted in the text.

The fantasy of identity through victimization, the search for use, becomes a structural metaphor that displays itself lavishly and has nothing to do with moral value or metaphysical possibility. It is no wonder then that the final trial in Elkin's novel deliberately pretends to offer a qualitative judgment but merely teases us with it; the verdict nullifies any potential moral or metaphysical contest between crowd and hero and leaves the novelist in solitary liberation, "free to plunder and profane" (p. 29), victorious over morality, philosophy, and his clutter of characters.

At the beginning of *A Bad Man* Feldman reveals, as almost his sole motivating anticipation of prison life, a curiosity to see if he is different from the others, all clearly stripped of families and social cares. What the final trial reveals, in the face of a conviction rigged by a spurious and secular god-warden and directed against a trivialized martyr muttering the classic tragic claim of innocence to a deaf universe, is that he is not different at all. There are no dynamics other than those of the novelist and his games. "The things you've charged me with," cries Feldman, "the masturbation, the bribes, my disdain for the place, almost everything—are all things you're guilty of yourselves" (p. 314). And the crowd answers: "Yes. That's so. Almost everything." "Doesn't that make a difference?" asks Feldman. And the answer is no. It means, instead, that Feldman is guilty of bearing false witness against himself. They are weary of his affectation of uniqueness in the use of spiels (the only conversations in the "games . . . of Feldman's Olympic friendship" [p. 331]), tired of his pretense that he has something they wish to hear or be affected or persuaded by. Feldman's demand for justice is far from the great revolutionary cry in Zola's *Germinal* for "Bread! Bread! Bread!" and from those feelings evoked by the philosophical recognition that Caesar and the chambermaid have the same soul, and that the king and the peasant share the same grave. The hero has become an echo of the crowd that no longer functions to test the sense of words, and the author, disjoined from both hero and crowd, is left to sink or swim in the flow of his own style.

Differentiation of the hero can finally be suffered neither by his author nor by the other characters, whether it be willed as in Feldman or natural as in Omensetter in William Gass's novel *Omensetter's Luck*. Omensetter is a vessel into which is poured all that others want themselves to be, but a post-lapsarian hero's fall teaches nothing. What can the fallen learn from the fall in a world more interested in destroying the relationships between men than in justifying the ways of God to man? While the "tellers" Tott, Pimber, and Furber expose their guilts and frustrations, their repressions and justifications, Omensetter, like E. M. Forster's "perfectly adjusted organism," is silent. He exists wholly in the present, with no need of a past for hoarding the soul's hangovers:

> What Omensetter did he did so simply that it seemed a miracle. It eased from him, his life did, like the smooth broad crayon line of the man who drew your cartoon at the fair. . . . Did he move so easily because, despite his size, he wasn't fat inside; he hadn't packed the past around his bones, or put his soul in suet.[35]

In the beginning he is cyclic like nature, elemental by birth, not by rebirth. Metaphor after metaphor links him to a natural climate: "Omensetter cast an interest like a shade" (p. 48). His clarity is to a fallen world a dark secret: "Omensetter put his head up in the stream where the wind blew away his words" (p. 69). "He was like a piece of weather in the room" (p. 235). What wills him into the mythic proportion of a great metaphysical threat is a world of artist-spies, composers of legends for the celebration of their only definition of reality. Tott, an auctioneer of stories, spiels to unwilling ears; Pimber is a soliloquizer of the self; and Furber talks with extraordinary eloquence in the graveyard to a ghost. Their marvelous words are not for listeners—they are self-sealing substitutes for density of life. Furber the lustful, the panty pincher only in fantasy, confesses: "Yes,

35. William Gass, *Omensetter's Luck* (New York: New American Library, 1966). Future references will be to this edition and will be noted in the text.

words were superior; they maintained a superior control; they touched without your touching; they were at once the bait, the hook, the line, the pole, and the water in between" (p. 138). What cannot be believed must be spoken; this is the compensation of the artist-spy. During Omensetter's rise, his period of grace, Furber is "inhabited, possessed" (p. 141); by Omensetter's fall, he goes mad. His vessel no longer can contain the words by which his own life can be sanctified.

The Ur-composer subdues conversation by words that flow so beautifully it seems "a miracle." Novelists like Bellow and Doris Lessing have less faith in the power of words to leap over moral barriers. Their Herzogs and Sammlers, their Annas, keep the unappeasing, self-mocking, and modest contracts with the old worlds of knowing and feeling, with the past's history; they testify to the humanist's fear of the miraculous metaphysics of words. Looking over their shoulders, these novelists recompose faces "through all the confusion and degraded clowning of this life through which we are speeding." [36] Their intellectual play and an almost totally mental scene cannot free them from the intransigent minds, hearts, and words of others.

At the end of her consciously "written" novel *Free Women*, Anna Wulf, who speaks with Lessing's voice in the exploratory energy of her notebooks, projects a response to the frustrations of illusory orders that would be high parody to the absurdist. A literary career, which for the humanist shares the inadequacies of all modes of organizing reality, yields to a less ambitious and more social approach, that of marriage-counseling and teaching. Her own problems with marriage might suggest that the choice is a travesty of purpose, but Anna refuses to let parody take advantage of her failures. Her choice has none of the absurdist glamor of inverse heroism or rebellion by masochistic reduction. The value of the role lies in its relaxed absorption of an inevitable irony, that "shadow of the third" which falls between visions of

36. Bellow, *Mr. Sammler's Planet*, p. 313.

order and our sense of chaos.[37] "Trying to write truth and realizing it's not true" (p. 233) is a particularly exasperating experience because one keeps the illusion that literature can somehow correct life. But, for the writer who refuses to compensate for failure by glamorizing lies with explosions of style, there can be no ritual status for the word. The humanist novelist duly tries on the costumes of ideology and climbs down from the stage to be shown his seat.

Myths of politics, psychoanalysis, literature, and marriage are forced to play the game of life, and as vulnerable life-styles in the notebooks they cannot win. Nor can any form. The exaggerated formal pattern is surely a humorous and desperate reminder of how hopeless and yet how necessary are illusions of order. The humanist's novel is no threat to God's creation. The insistence on being normal is anything but a consoling compulsion, but it guarantees companionship. The acceptance of the "long littleness of life" (p. 366) and of the novelist's struggle is not an impressive heroism, but it gathers in the reader.

The novelist-heroine is quick to feel the political and moral pressure on fiction either to tell the truth or to become superfluous. Anna of the notebooks dramatizes the pressure by consistently complaining about the modern separation of personality from philosophy. The separation of Anna's novel from the notebooks is an illustration of this divorce and a reminder that the novel cannot magically heal this disintegration. Retrospective fiction, which Sartre calls anachronistic, seems to Anna to be nostalgia because it depends so heavily on the recollection of personality in tranquillity.[38] The re-creation of the Mashopi years

37. Doris Lessing, *The Golden Notebook* (New York: Simon & Schuster, 1962), p. 262. Future references will be to this edition and will be noted in the text. "Shadow of the third" is used as a title for Anna's novel about Ella; it relates to a triangular tension that strains all symmetries in life and haunts conscious form with threatened breakups. Anna's attitude here is comparable to Nietzsche's in his preface to "Ecce Homo": "I do not refute ideals; all I do is to draw on my gloves in their presence" (p. 135).
38. See Jean-Paul Sartre's discussion of the novel's situation in 1947 in *What Is Literature?*, trans. Bernard Frechtman (New York: Philosophical Library, 1949), p. 224.

in "The Black Notebook" has, nevertheless, a secret and un-
declared power, which in large part counteracts the political and
moralistic condemnations of personality's embarrassment. If the
"form of nostalgia" [39] seems thin, the repressed and uninspired
ordering of the Ella novel in "The Yellow Notebook" seems
evasive and cheating as it sorts the colors of memory and, like
psychoanalysis, begins to raise experience to a desiccated myth.
The representative dimensions of personality pretend to be sufficient. In despair at this evasion, Anna turns to her diary; but
that is even more inadequate because it pretends not to be fiction,
and logic does not render the truth of character:

> So all that is a failure too. The Blue Notebook, which I had
> expected to be the most truthful of the notebooks, is worse than
> any of them. I expected a terse record of facts to present some
> sort of a pattern when I read it over, but this sort of record is
> as false as the account of what happened on the 15th of Sep-
> tember, 1954, which I read now embarrassed because of its
> emotionalism and because of its assumption that if I wrote "at
> nine-thirty I went to the lavatory to shit and at two to pee and
> at four I sweated," this would be more real than if I simply
> wrote what I thought (p. 400).

What are we to do with the inability of tones and styles to render us in our times?

The pure moments of apocalyptic madness, when we manage
to rise to an order of knowing outside of history, tell the humanist that we cannot escape by or from words any more than from
time. The wild climax of "The Golden Notebook" section is
contained in a novel called *The Golden Notebook*, which records
the story of shared limitations and testifies to necessary compromises in form and style. In the climactic "projectionist" scene of
"The Golden Notebook" section (Anna had often considered
the film's memory the finest) Anna admits:

---

39. This is Anna's term for the form and style of the Mashopi episode
(see p. 196).

Words. Words. I play with words, hoping that some combination, even a chance combination will say what I want. Perhaps better with music? But music attacks my inner ear like an antagonist, it's not my world. The fact is, the real experience can't be described. I think bitterly that a row of asterisks, like an old-fashioned novel, might be better. Or a symbol of some kind, a circle perhaps, or a square. Anything at all, but not words. The people who have been there, in the place in themselves where words, patterns, order, dissolve, will know what I mean and the others won't. But once having been there, there's a terrible irony, a terrible shrug of the shoulders, and it's not a question of fighting it, or disowning it, or of right or wrong, but simply knowing it is there, always. It's a question of bowing to it, so to speak, with a kind of courtesy, as to an ancient enemy: All right, I know you are there, but we have to preserve the forms, don't we? And perhaps the condition of your existing at all is precisely that we preserve the forms, create the patterns—have you thought of that? (p. 542).

This hardly startling news is a strange compensation. If the word cannot realize the shadow of the third, neither can the shadow be reached on any extension but that of verbal approximation. The humanist reluctantly but necessarily submits aesthetic transcendence to the same irony that checks moral purity; the presence of the first and second shadows, our standard relationships, makes victory of commonplace. This double action prevents us from being, for any length of time, comfortable and special victims of history.

Leventhal's hoarding of spirit, while accepted as historically justified, is a sanctioned response to the modern decomposition of values, the crumbling of agreed views on the universe. It is a way of preserving energy. Anna frequently attempts to hypothesize from the notion that society is "dead or dying" (p. 467). In such a millenium, feeling must be open to adulteration:

It is possible that in order to keep love, feeling, tenderness alive, it will be necessary to feel these emotions ambiguously, even for what is false and debased, or for what is still an idea, a shadow in the willed imagination only . . . or if what we feel is pain, then we must feel it, acknowledging that the alternative is death. Better anything than the shrewd, the calculated, the noncommittal, the refusal of giving for fear of the consequences (p. 467).

She censures the soul's hibernation, but her complaint is sentimental. The times have not made love more difficult. When Anna fights against Mrs. Marks's leveling of her unique historical situation, she protests:

> They didn't look at themselves as I do. They didn't feel as I do. How could they? I don't want to be told when I wake up, terrified by a dream of total annihilation, because of the H-bomb exploding, that people felt that way about the crossbow. It isn't true. There is something new in the world. And I don't want to hear, when I've had encounter with some Mogul in the film industry, who wields the kind of power over men's minds that no emperor ever did, and I come back feeling trampled on all over, that Lesbia felt like that after an encounter with her wine-merchant (p. 404).

Her rage touches us by its awareness of how vulnerable our personal measure is to habits of historical expansion and reduction, how impossible it is to use the times without feeling used by them. We see dreams of total annihilation and golden ages through the "crack" across personality (p. 405). The dreams are not dismissed, nor is any philosophy or politics irrelevant to personality; but they are never expressive of individual character. The novel has one advantage over philosophy—it knows it is merely a temporary place in which personality can grasp for a history. The individualizing memory yearns for consoling orders of form and cause. But while it stays in provisional times, as it must, it can never be pure or fix its own anxieties.

Though not exuberant like Gide's, Anna's parodies of style that attempt to set personality by a consistent tone and form are signs of health rather than symptoms of desperation. She continually assumes the burden of criticizing her own escape into abstractions by marking the parody in every word she writes.

Early in the notebooks, when she talks about the "anti-humanist bullying" concerning "evaporation of the personality" (p. 99), she will not let the frail characters of fiction be overcome by the cultural facts of anonymity. Memory does not merely evoke; it re-creates within time a particular tree, a particular face:

> Suppose I were to meet Maryrose now, all these years later, she'd make some gesture, or turn her eyes in such a way, and there she'd be, Maryrose and indestructible. Or suppose she "broke down," or became mad. She would break down into her components, and the gesture, the movement of the eyes would remain, even though some connection had gone (p. 99).

So physical is the remembrance, that Anna suggests that the film rather than the novel might be a better agent of translation: "What business has a novelist to cling to the memory of a smile or a look, knowing so well the complexities behind them?" But there is a stubborn attraction between the approximating word and the pictures of memory. Anna implies that it has something to do with the impossibility of opening the memory to fiction without fiction's inclusion of the remembering self. The word, like the writer, continually laughs at its own limitations, its necessity to express the soul by a smile. By so doing, it makes a story out of personality.

In retrospect the novelist-heroine worries about personality's cavalier neglect of morality:

> But the point is, and it is the point that obsesses me, . . . once I say that words like good, bad, strong, weak, are irrelevant, I am accepting amorality, and I do accept it the moment I start to write "a story," "a novel," because I simply don't care. All I care about is that I should describe Willi and Maryrose so that a reader can feel their reality (p. 67).

We come back to the old humanist transvaluation, that the real precedes the moral and guarantees it. The future of Anna in her novel *Free Women* indicates her instinct to continue the process of decomposing "fantastic" facades of morality, including that of

literature, to expose the faces behind them. The known is demoted to the tentative, and all healing is a provisional act. The
humanist, like the Sisyphus of both Camus and Lessing, is a boul-
der-pusher (p. 529), and his novel is the record of his recapitu-
lations. In one of the most moving passages in the novel, Lessing
has Anna superimpose Ella's fiction upon her own life; by this
extension, and inevitable retraction, of memory the novel keeps
feeling alive. By asking more of the novel we can drop it from
the mountain of purgatory into the brimstone of truth:

> The idea for this story intrigued me, and I began thinking how
> it should be written. How, for instance, would it change if I
> used Ella instead of myself? I had not thought about Ella for
> some time, and I realised that of course she had changed in the
> interval; she would have become more defensive, for instance.
> I saw her with her hair altered—she would be tying it back
> again, looking severe; she would be wearing different clothes.
> I was watching Ella moving about my room; and then I began
> imagining how she would be with Saul—much more intelligent,
> I think, than I, cooler, for instance. After a while I realised I
> was doing what I had done before, creating "the third"—the
> woman altogether better than I was. For I could positively mark
> the point where Ella left reality, left how she would, in fact,
> behave because of her nature; and move into a large generosity
> of personality impossible to her. But I didn't dislike this new
> person I was creating; I was thinking that quite possibly these
> marvellous, generous things we walk side by side with in our
> imaginations could come into existence, simply because we need
> them, because we imagine them. Then I began to laugh be-
> cause of the distance between what I was imagining and what
> in fact I was, let alone what Ella was (p. 545).

To mock what we imagine keeps us rich in self-irony.

✳ EPILOGUE ✳

I N A DIALOGUE with George Duthuit, Beckett exhibits an impatience with art, however bold, that remains "a certain order on the plane of the feasible." [1] When Duthuit asks what other plane there is, Beckett replies:

> Logically none. Yet I speak of an art turning from it in disgust, weary of its puny exploits, weary of pretending to be able, of being able, of doing a little better the same old thing, of going a little further along a dreary road.

Duthuit then asks him what he prefers. Beckett responds:

> The expression that there is nothing to express, nothing with which to express, nothing from which to express, no desire to express, together with the obligation to express.

Beckett has pushed the Flaubertian retreat to its ultimate barriers. The word, freed from occasion, can celebrate the dying of itself,

1. Samuel Beckett, "Three Dialogues," in *Samuel Beckett: A Collection of Critical Essays,* ed. Martin Esslin (Englewood Cliffs, N.J.: Prentice-Hall, 1965), pp. 16–22.

restoration of the innocence of silence, only by celebrating the dying of experience. Because the humanist remains on the plane of the endurable, his novels are not of man's tragic martyrdom; they record man's inevitable necessity to express his comic nature. The humanist pulls the words of the absurdist down from their lofty purity and lowers them to his own parasitic fictions, which are meant neither to survive nor to replace the world.

 INDEX

Absurd: defined, 6; recognition of, in literary humanism, 6, 8
Absurdist: abstraction, use of, 5, 6, 92; aesthetic transcendence, use of, 16, 18, 113; apocalyptic temper of, 13; audience, separation from, 17, 18; character, use of, 18, 24, 26; confession, use of, 16; deceit as truth, use of, 7, 8; defined, 6; eccentricity of, 11, 12; exhibitionism of, 11; expectation of ultimate truth, 7, 92, 111; history, use of, 13, 14, 15; isolation of, 11–12, 16, 115; literature as exorcism, use of, 10, 13, 14; martyrdom of, 10, 24; nonnovelistic humanist, common ground with, 5–6; perfection, demand for, 9, 10; as reflection of new order, xi; self-justification of, 9; self-punishment of, 10; wit, use of, 9
Anderson, Quentin, 55 n
Arnold, Matthew, 50 n

Barth, John, 123, 124, 126
Beckett, Samuel, 110, 112, 113, 114, 115 n, 124, 137
Bellow, Saul, xi, 17 n, 117–22, 130, 133

Bersani, Leo, 115 n

Camus, Albert, 6, 8, 17, 69–70, 89 n, 91, 108, 109, 118, 136
Crews, Frederick, 79 n, 83 n

Dickens, Charles, 95 n
Diderot, Denis, 104
Dostoevsky, Fyodor, xii, 4–9, 13, 17, 28, 29, 110, 117, 118, 120, 125, 126; abstraction, rejection of, 87, 89, 90, 91–92, 93, 96; absurd, recognition of, 6, 93; absurdist attitude in nonfiction of, 95–100; act superior to word in, 86, 92; apocalyptic temper, rejection of, 88–89, 90, 92; Camus, Albert, compared with, 108–9; Eliot, George, compared with, 93 n, 95, 97; Flaubert, Gustave, compared with, 35; Forster, E. M., compared with, 85; history, use of, in service of novel's humanism, 90; humanist attitude in novels of, 85–105; humanitarianism, rejection of, 86, 92, 94, 99; metaphysics, use of, as rejection of absolute solutions, 86, 87, 89, 90, 92; parody, use of conversation by gesture in, 85, 86; psy-

139

The text of this book is set in ten-point Janson, two points leaded. The display type is Perpetua, italic and roman. S. D. Warren manufactured the paper, an antique stock; Holliston Mills, the binding fabric, a meadow-green Crown Linen. The book was composed, printed, and bound by Kingsport Press, Inc., Kingsport, Tennessee. Typography and binding design are by Elizabeth G. Stout.